The Uke Buke
Learn to Play Slack Key Style 'Ukulele
by Mark Kailana Nelson

Musical examples available for download at www.mark-o.com.

ISBN-013: 978-1456422097
ISBN-10: 145642209X
© 2010 Acme Arts • PO Box 967 • Jacksonville OR 97530.
Duplication, save for personal use, is both a crime and a serious hit on your karma. Or a sin, if that's your world view. Or, to be formal about it:
All rights for publication and distribution are reserved. No part of this book may be reproduced in any form or by any electronic, digital or mechanical means including information storage and retrieval systems without permission in writing from the publisher.

Copyright disclaimer: Determining copyrights in Hawaiian songs is not always easy. Sadly many songs fell into the public domain through faulty registration or incomplete record-keeping. We have made every effort to track down and secure permission to use these songs. If we have inadvertently published a previously copyrighted composition without permission, we advise the copyright owners to contact us so that we may give credit in future editions.

Aloha

It is no secret that the Hawaiians fell in love with the 'ukulele the first time they heard it. Within just a few short years after three Portuguese immigrants brought the modest little instrument on that long sea voyage, Hawaiian musicians took the world by storm.

No trade exposition, Vaudeville review or whistle stop concert tour was complete without a bevy of exotic hula maidens swaying to the tropical sounds of the steel guitar and 'ukulele.

Why, Hawaiian music without an 'ukulele is almost unthinkable!

Here is a collection of classic Hawaiian melodies arranged for solo 'ukulele, slack key style. What's that? Slack key–or *kī ho'alu*– is a melodic, finger-picked guitar style created by Hawaiian *paniolo* in the mid-19th Century. The call it "Hawaiian soul music," so dear is it to the hearts of the Island born.

It is only natural that some 'ukulele players in Hawai'i would re-tune their instruments and play in that style. I first heard it many years ago when I was invited to a wonderful Maui jam session. I'd never heard any one play the 'ukulele like that–pure chicken skin! I asked my friend how he got that beautiful sound, he smiled and said "Slack Key!"

That inspired me to adapt slack key guitar stylings to the 'ukulele and to share the music with you. I hope you will agree that it sure sounds sweet.

Mark Kailana Nelson
Applegate Valley, Oregon

Who This Book Is For

If you love your 'ukulele, can play chords in the first position and you want to try your hand at playing melodies, this book is for you. That is not to say it won't be a bit of a challenge for some. But what is life if not an adventure?

Many uke players in Hawai'i favor the larger concert and tenor sized instruments. Why? The larger body lets the strings sustain and the longer scale length makes it easier to finger chords and melodies up the neck. Likewise, to increase the melodic range even further, they swap out the high G on the fourth string for one an octave lower.

Although some of the more basic arrangements can be played on any 'ukulele in standard tuning, you will need to restring with a low G to get the most out of this book. And you will get even more enjoyment on a tenor uke.

So now you have an excuse to buy another 'ukulele. Tell 'em it's my fault.

Table of Contents

How This Book is Organized 4
TAB and Musical Notation 5
   Lesson: Common Hawaiian Turnarounds 10

Section One: Arrangements in Standard Tuning 12

Pūpū Hinuhinu 13
‘Ulupalakua 14
Ahe Lau Makani 16
Iesu Me Ke Kanaka Waiwai 18

Section Two: Slack Key ‘Ukulele Solos 20

   Lesson: How to Play Slack Key ‘Ukulele 21
Kealoha 22
‘Ukulele Slack Key #1, Basic Version 24
   Lesson: Taropatch Turnarounds & Double Stops 26
Salomila 30
Papakolea 32
Mauna Loa 33
Aloha ‘Oe 34
Ahe Lau Makani 36
‘Ukulele Slack Key #1, second version 38
   Lesson: How to Change Keys 40
Pūpū Hinuhinu 42
Kowali 43
He Aloha No‘o Honolulu 44
Hi‘ilawe 46
   Lesson: C Wahine Tuning 49
Paniolo Slack 50
   Lesson: Slack Key Style in Standard Tuning 53
Iesu Me Ke Kanaka Waiwai 54

Section Three: Advanced Slack Key Style Arrangements 57

Moana Chimes 58
Kimo's Slack Key 59
Hula Blues 60
‘Ukulele Dream Slack Key 62
Makee Ailana 65
Ahe Lau Makani, extended version 66
Medley: Slack Key Hula/Kowali/Pauoa Liko Ka Lehua 70
‘Ulupalakua, Slack Key Style 74
Iesu Me Ke Kanaka Waiwai, Slack Key Style 77
‘Ukulele Slack Key #1, extended version 82

Guide to Hawaiian Pronunciation 86
Resources 87
About the Author 88

How This Book Is Organized

As with my previous book, "Learn to Play Fingerstyle Solos for 'Ukulele," (Mel Bay Publications), the songs are arranged more or less in ascending order of difficulty. If you start at the beginning and work your way to the back you will gain a thorough understanding of how to play slack key style 'ukulele.

Of course, if you are the adventurous type—and what 'ukulele player isn't?—just dive in.

The first section features fairly easy arrangements in standard re-entrant 'ukulele tuning. (That's "My - Dog - Has - Fleas" tuning to you.) For those of you unfamiliar with playing melody on the uke, I've included playing notes and some fingering hints. Take time to get to know these classic melodies; I return to them several times over the course of the book to illustrate various techniques and arranging concepts.

Next comes a group of tunes arranged for slack key 'ukulele. Most of the arrangements are fairly short; I want you to build up a basic repertoire of tunes and techniques before delving into the more complex arrangements.

The final section consists of new material in advanced arrangements including extended versions of some of the tunes we've already explored. Many of these songs have intros, bridges and a coda, and feature more difficult fingerings, slurs and the like.

I have scattered lessons and exercises throughout the book to introduce new tunings and concepts and to prepare you for the music to come.

My goal is not only to teach you a number of classic Hawaiian melodies, but to show you *why* I made the decisions I made so that you can begin to create your own arrangements.

To play the slack key style arrangements in Sections Two and Three you will need to outfit your instrument with a low G, or 4th string. You can purchase low G string sets at any large music store or online retailer that has a good selection of quality 'ukulele. While you are shopping, why not pick up a new tenor uke, too? The longer scale and increased body size really helps.

All of the arrangements in this book are my own work and are © 2010 acme arts. Feel free to share your playing with your friends, but please do not duplicate the music without permission.

A word about Baritone 'Ukulele:

You can play any of the arrangements in this book on a baritone instrument simply by playing the Tab as written. Of course, the pitches will be different, and you'll need to transpose the chords if you are playing with someone else. If you'd like to play in the same keys as the music is written, simply capo at the fifth fret.

TAB and Musical Notation

All of the music is written in standard notation and Tablature for 'ukulele.

Tablature, or TAB, is an ancient system of musical notation in which lines represent the instrument's strings. Tunings are given as pitches immediately to the left of the first line.

Fingering positions are indicated by numbers. TAB doesn't give any indication of how long to hold each note; for that refer to the staff above the TAB. (If you are unfamiliar with standard musical notation, keep reading.)

Note that the strings are numbered starting with the string closest to the floor, so in standard uke tuning, A is the first string, E the second, C the third and G the fourth. As you can see from the example below, TAB reverses the apparent order of the strings. Don't ask me why.

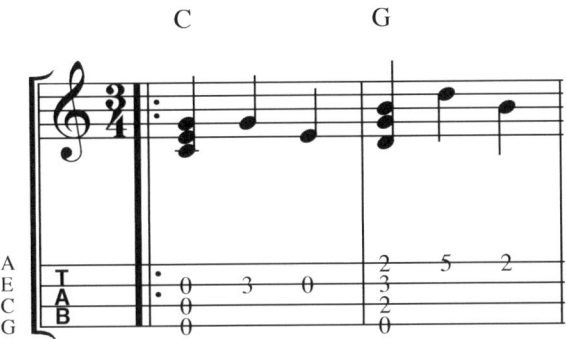

In this example you would play the open second, third and first strings on beat one, fret the second string on the third fret and then the open second string. In the second measure, start with a G chord, then reach up to the fifth fret on the first string and finish back at the second fret, first string.

Right hand fingerings have not been indicated: experiment with different fingerings to see what works best for you. In general, I place my thumb on the fourth string, index on the third, middle on the second and ring finger on the first string when playing chords and basic fingerstyle arrangements.

For arrangements with an alternating bass pattern, I play both the third and fourth strings (and sometimes the second) with my thumb.

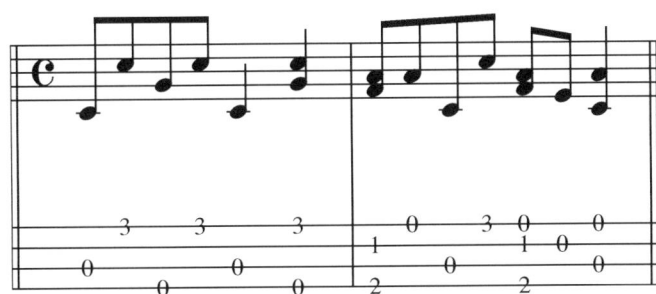

Here are some more TAB symbols and playing techniques you will encounter.

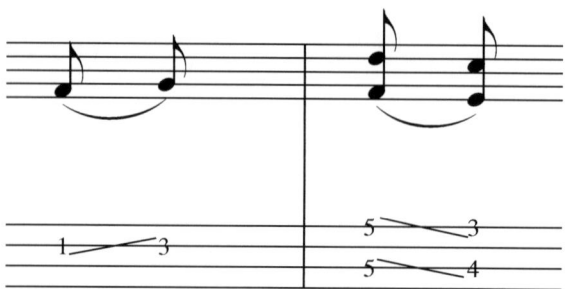

Slide: Pick the first note—or notes—and then slide up or down to the second. Be sure to give each note its full time value!

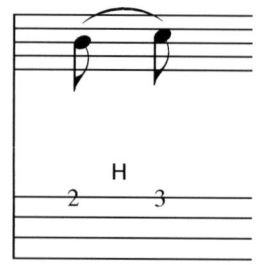

Hammer-on: Play the first note, then rapidly press your finger down to the fretboard to sound the second note.

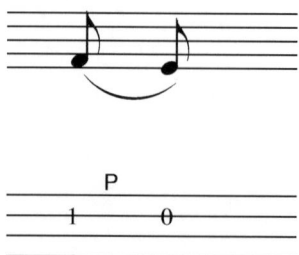

Pull-off: Play the first note, then quickly pull off your finger to sound the lower note.

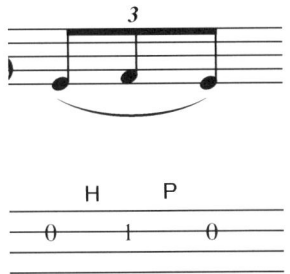

Hammer/pull combination: A common feature of slack key, this is a rapid combination of a hammer-on and pull-off executed as a quick flick of the finger.

Harmonic: Also called chimes in Hawaiian music. Lightly touch the string directly over the fret to produce a ringing tone. Try moving your plucking hand back towards the bridge slightly to better define the harmonic.

One more thing: You can often tell how to finger a given measure by looking ahead and "collapsing" the individual notes into chords or double stops.
For instance, this:

is played out of these positions:

Although it is not necessary to know how to read musical notation to play the songs in this book, knowledge of a few musical symbols will greatly enhance your enjoyment.

Since the TAB will give you the correct pitches on a properly tuned instrument, you really only have to worry about the rhythm of a particular piece.

Music is divided into **measures**, each of which contains the number of beats delineated by the **time signature:**

 4/4 means four beats per measure, each quarter note counts as one beat.

 3/4 is three beats per measure, each quarter note counts as one beat.

Occasionally alternate symbols are used for the time signature. **Cut Time** (¢) is another way of writing 2/2; and **Common Time** (C) is the same as 4/4.

Each beat can be further divided into smaller and smaller units:

o   The longest note is the whole note; it is the equivalent of four quarter notes, or four counts.

𝅗𝅥   The half note is equal to two quarter notes.

♩   The quarter note gets one count.

♪   Two eighth notes equals a quarter note.

𝅘𝅥𝅯   The sixteenth note is half as long as the eighth note; so two sixteenths equal one eighth, four sixteenths equal a quarter, and sixteen equal a whole note.

Rests correspond to each of the different note values.

o = —   𝅗𝅥 = ▬   ♩ = 𝄽   ♪ = 𝄾   𝅘𝅥𝅯 = 𝄿

A dot placed next to a note (or rest) lengthens it by one half of its value. For example:

♩. = ♪♪♪

Ties are used for notes that are held for their combined values.

 This figure would be held as long as three eighth notes.

Triplets are groups of three notes that are played in the space of two.

For example, three eighth note triplets

would be played in the same amount of time as two eighth notes.

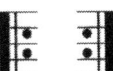 **Repeat signs**: repeat the enclosed phrase one time before going on to the next one.

|1 | This sign means play the measures under the sign on the first time through and then go back to the beginning of the section. On the repeat you skip over the first ending and play the second ending.

⌒ A **fermata** is the symbol to hold a note just a little longer than its value. It is used to add expression to your playing.

D.C. From the Italian, **Da Capo**, meaning "Head." This sign directs you to go back to the beginning of the music. **D.C. al Fine** directs you to play from the beginning to the designated end of the song.

D.S. **Dal Segno**, or "to the sign," tells you to look for the symbol (𝄋) and play that section next rather than returning to the beginning. **D.S. al Coda** means play from the sign to the coda sign, then jump to the coda.

⊕ A **Coda** sign is often used to mark the ending of the piece. When you see this sign, skip down to the section marked ⊕ **Coda** to finish the song. Coda is Italian for "Tail," by the way.

Rit. Also **Ritard.** Gradually slow the pace to bring the music to a graceful conclusion.

Getting Started

One of the defining characteristics of Hawaiian music is an extra one or two measure turnaround–a simple movement from the dominant chord back to the tonic. So typical is this that steel guitar players refer to it as "the Hawaiian Vamp." In fact, all you have to do is play a few of these examples to be instantaneously transported under the palms at Waikiki.

Common Hawaiian 'Ukulele Turnarounds

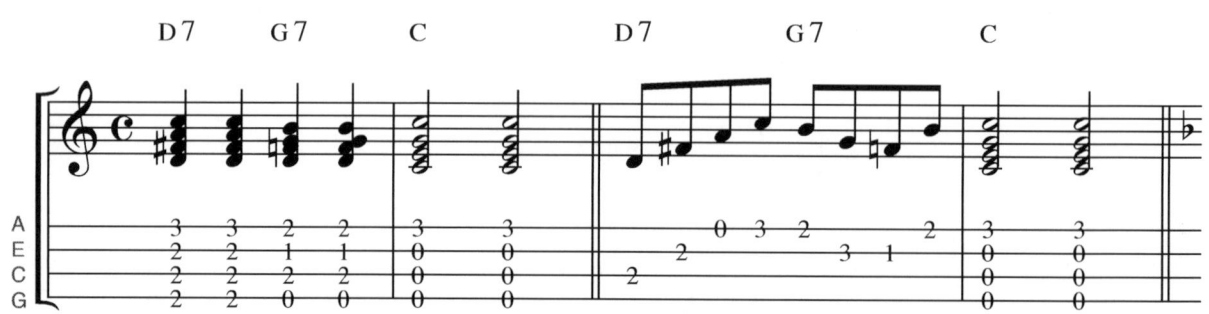

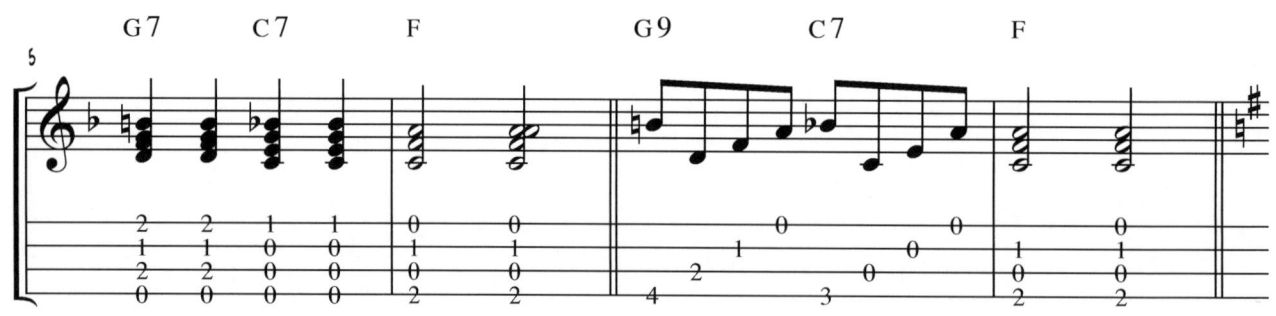

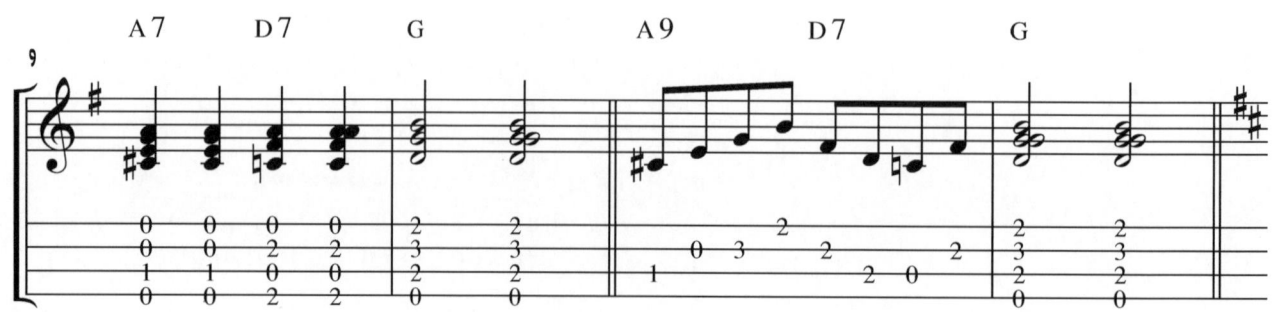

A Note About Tempo

Hawaiian music can be played a wide variety of tempos, depending on the song, the mood of the performer, or the time of day. For this reason I have decided not to suggest metronome markings for any of the arrangements that follow.

Some songs, like *Aloha 'Oe*, sound best at a stately tempo; others, notably *'Ulupalakua*, can be played as fast as your fingers will let you fly.

For the most part, let your heart and your ears determine the tempo. You can never go wrong if you play slowly and with a slight tropical swing!

Section One
Arrangements in Standard 'Ukulele Tuning

The first few arrangements in the book are all fairly simple, from there things get a little more difficult. If you are new to playing melody, I have given notes on fingerings for the first two songs to help you get started.

You will return to each of these melodies in several different arrangements over the course of the book, so take some time to get to know them. Listen for the essential melody, notice how the harmonies move.

After you have progressed to the more difficult stylings, check back to see how slack key style differs from solo 'ukulele playing.

Pūpū Hinuhinu

Nona Beamer

Pūpū Hinuhinu. or Shiny Shells, is a delightful children's song written by Aunty Nona Beamer. I have indicated the finger positions with standard block chord diagrams to help get you started.

Play only the notes indicated. Try different right hand fingerings; you might sound the chords as quick rolls using your thumb and fingers or perhaps with an upward or downward strum.

When you reach the end, be sure to let your 'ukulele ring.

ʻUlupalakua

trad

Performance Notes

'Ulupalakua (Breadfruit Ripened on the Back) celebrates the beautiful ranchland on the uplands of Haleakalā, Maui.

This simple arrangement follows the vocal melody closely. Later on you will get the chance to play a full-throttle arrangement in slack key style.

Measures 1 & 2: Hold down the G chord for both of these measures, even when you are only playing single notes. So, for the open string at the end of Measure 1, you simply lift off one finger. You can either strum the chords, or play with a quick roll of the thumb and fingers.

Measure 3: Not much support for the melody here. Why? If you were to play a complete C chord, the melody would get lost because our ears always gravitate to the highest pitch. Note the syncopation.

Measure 7: You can hold a D7 chord for much of this measure. Playing out of chord positions helps connect the notes with one another.

Measures 9 & 10: Here's one version of the famous "Hawaiian Vamp."

Kaulana mai nei
A'o 'Ulupalakua
He 'īnikiniki ahiahi
Ka home a'o paniolo

E wehi e ku'u lei
A'o 'Ulupalakua
'Onaona me ka 'awapuhi
He nani ma'oli nō

Ha'ina mai ka puana
A'o 'Ulupalakua
He 'īnikiniki ahiahi
Ka home a'o paniolo

Famous
Is 'Ulupalakua
The the cold evening air pinches the skin
The home of the cowboys

My lei is an adornment
Of 'Ulupalakua
The sweet scent of ginger is
Truly beautiful

Tell the refrain
Of 'Ulupalakua
The the cold evening air pinches the skin
The home of the cowboy

Ahe Lau Makani

Standard uke tuning

Queen Liliʻuokalani

Ahe Lau Makani

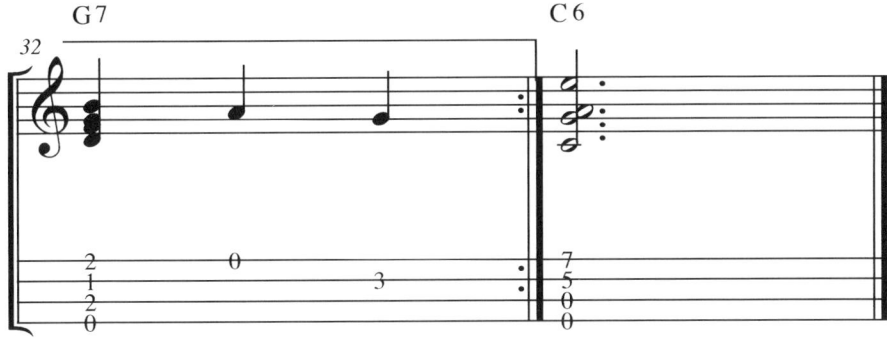

The title refers to a tropical breeze that gently stirs the leaves. You may either strum the chords or play them as rapid rolls.

Iesu Me Ke Kanaka Waiwai

standard tuning

John K. Almeida

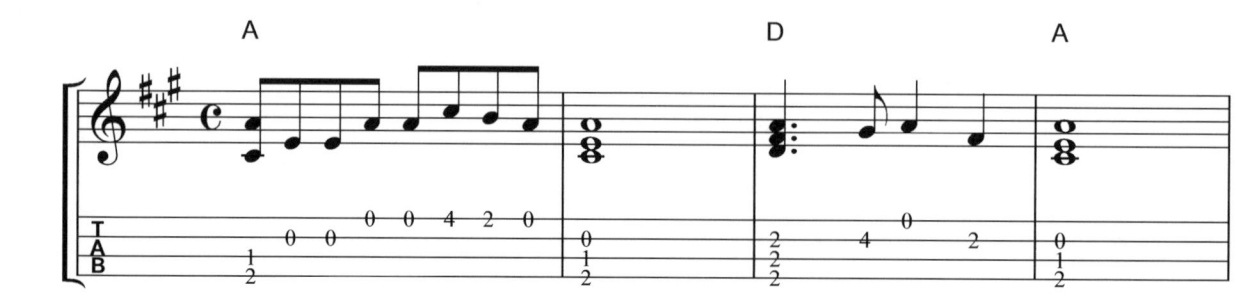

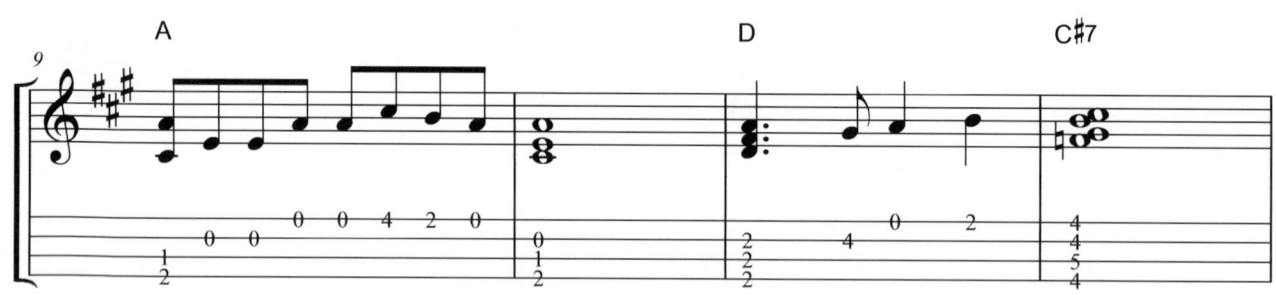
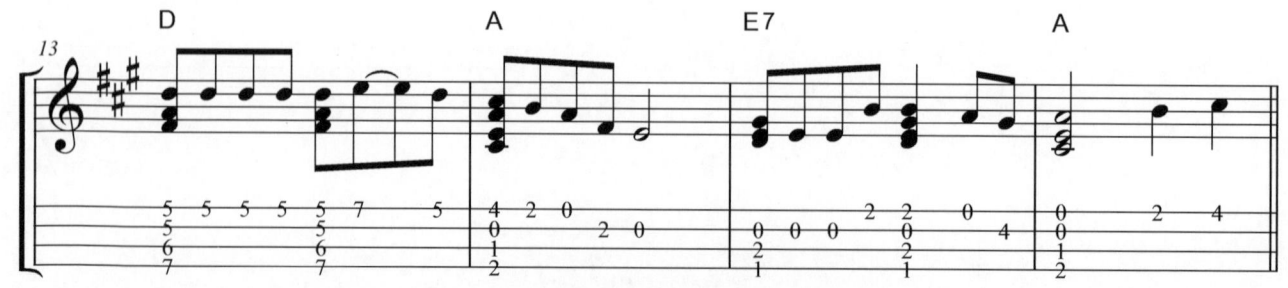

© 2010 Acme Arts. All Rights Reserved

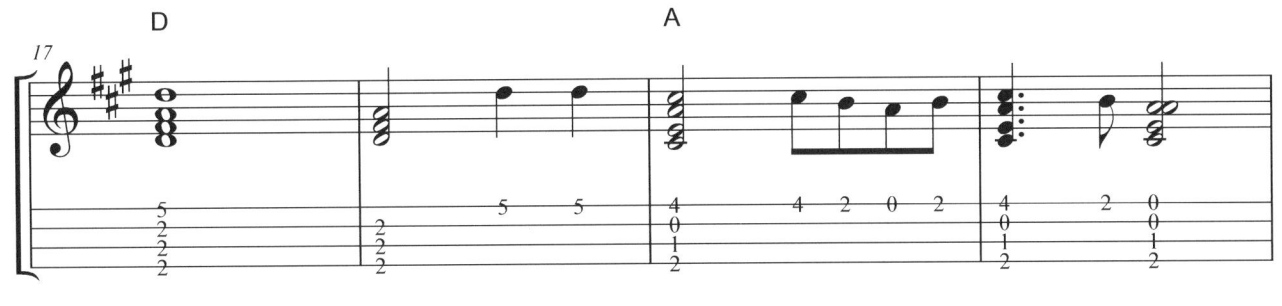
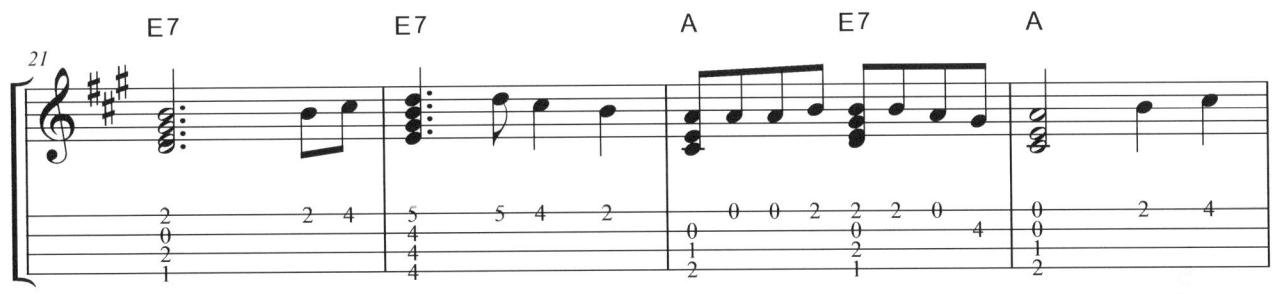
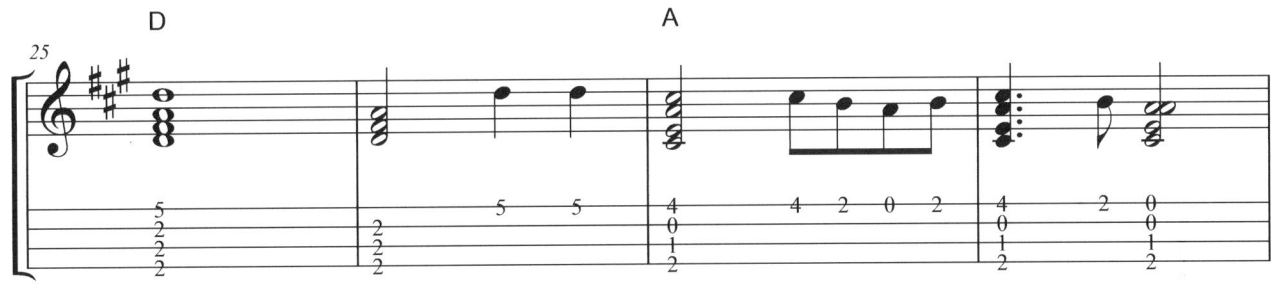
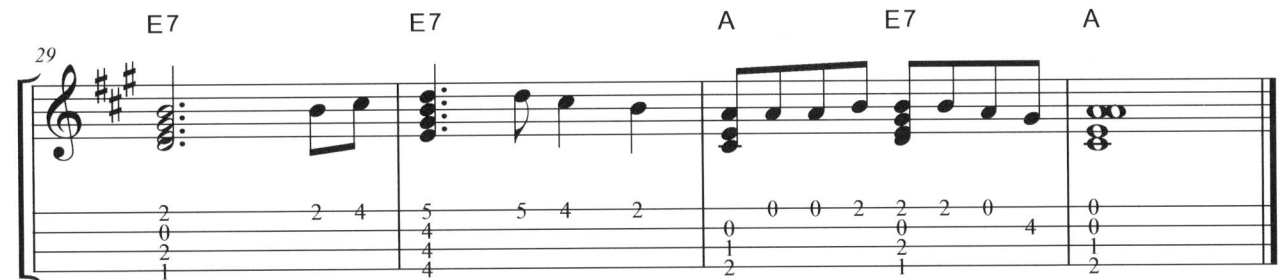

Johnny Almeida was one of Hawaii's most prolific composers. He wrote this song based on the Biblical story of Jesus and the rich man. We will return to this beautiful melody several times over the course of the book.

As before, play the chords using a rolling motion starting with your thumb.

Section Two
Slack Key Style

Slack key guitar, or *kī ho'alu*, developed in the rural Hawai'i of the 19th Century. Although it is a highly individualistic style—no two players approach the same song the same way—it does have certain readily identifiable characteristics.

The Hawaiian name means "loosen the key"; it refers to twisting the tuning keys on the guitar to create new, open tunings. But simply retuning the instrument does not make it slack key. Rather, slack key is a style and a repertoire. Some may even say that slack key is a culture, and who am I to argue?

Stylistically, slack key music employs a clear statement of melody and harmony on the treble strings, supported by a strong bass. A noted Big Island guitarist once chided my early attempts at playing Hawaiian style by stating, "It's not slack key if I cannot hear the bass!"

That begs the question: without the bass range of a guitar, is it even possible to play slack key on the 'ukulele? Some say yes, some say no. But Sheldon Brown of Maui makes no bones about it, he calls his playing "slack key" and that is good enough for me.

So what else makes slack key sound the way it does? Mostly it is the way the player phrases the melody, adding subtle syncopation, hammer-ons, pull-offs and slides, harmonies based on thirds and sixths and slippery Island-style licks that make you feel like you are sitting in the shade on a coral-strewn beach as gentle trade winds whisper a love song to the palms.

Over the next few pages, you will learn the basics of playing slack key on your 'ukulele. The first few songs will get you familiar with re-tuning, playing alternating bass, and how to add a tropical lilt to your playing.

Ready to dig in to some classic Hawaiian melodies?

How to Play Slack Key ʻUkulele

The first thing you will need to is replace the standard high G fourth string with one an octave lower. You can purchase low G ʻukulele strings at most music stores, or online. In a pinch, pick up a single nylon guitar G (or third string) and cut it down to size. You may need to widen the slots at the nut and bridge of your uke; if you are unsure about how to do this consult a competent repair tech.

As I said earlier, you might find that a larger instrument like a tenor or concert uke makes playing up the neck easier. What is more, a longer scale length makes chimes–or harmonics–really sing.

The most common slack key guitar tuning is called Taropatch–no one knows why–and features a G major chord on the top three strings: G-B-D. Transposed to the ʻukulele, the tuning becomes a C major chord.

From standard tuning, lower the first string one whole step, from an A to a G. This gives the pitches of G-C-E-G, starting on the fourth string.

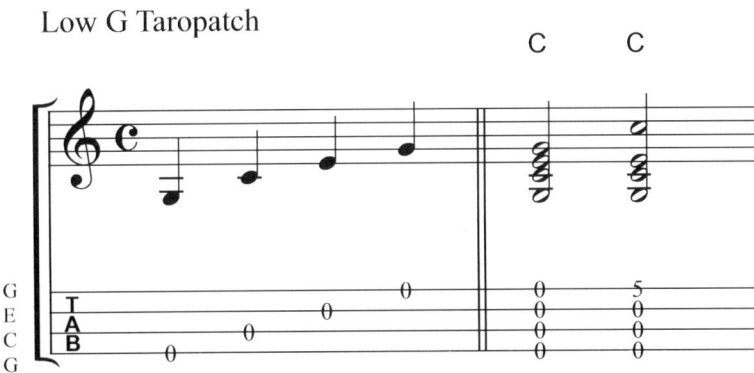

Note: if you haven't swapped out for a low G string, your first and fourth strings will be exactly the same pitch instead of an octave apart.

The first two arrangements in this section are designed to teach you the basics of the style, so take some time with them before you move on to the instructional material on page 26.

Kealoha
Slack Key Style

Ida & Akoni Malacas

Low G Taropatch Tuning

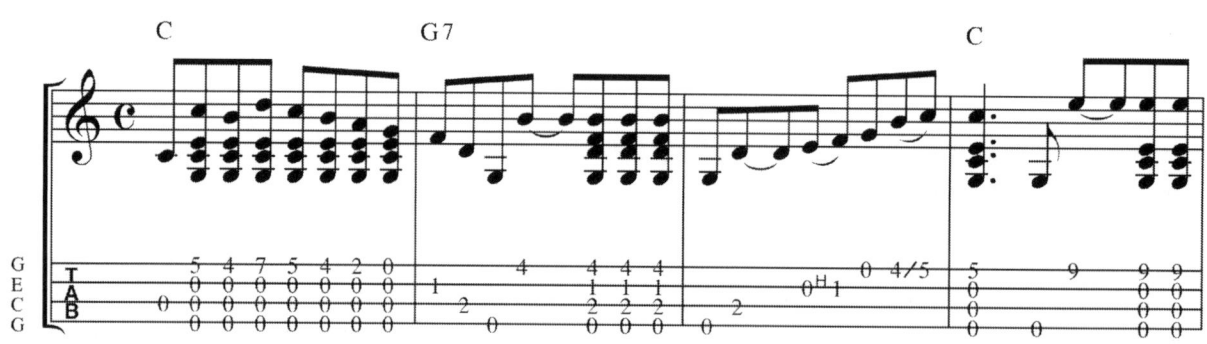

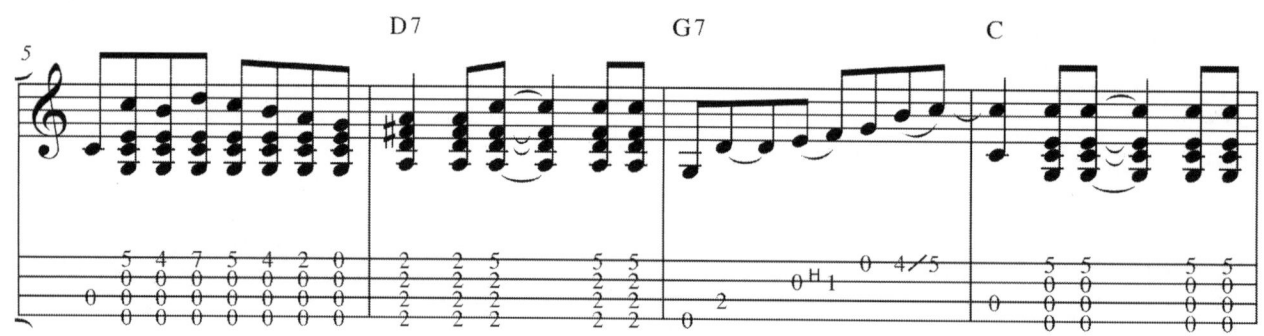

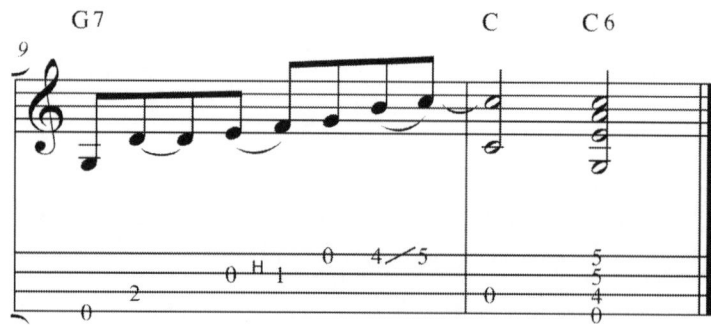

Performance Notes

Kealoha – "Beloved" – is a beautiful melody and a slack key guitar standard. Before you start playing, take a look at the TAB. Notice that three measures, numbers 3, 7 and 9, are all exactly the same. Ditto measures 1 and 5 are also the same. That sure cuts down on the amount of material to learn!

Measure 1: Play the open C string with your thumb. I use a gentle up and down strum to play the rest of the measure, taking care that the melody notes on the first string are clear.

Measure 2: The melody notes outline a G7 chord. Note that the fingering is slightly different from a G7 in standard tuning. You have to compensate for the retuned first string!

Measure 3: I start with the chord from the previous measure to play this; lifting up individual fingers when I need an open string. Pick the open fourth string with your thumb and use your fingers for everything else. Notice how you slide into the C on the fifth fret just ahead of the downbeat of the next measure.

This measure utilizes a very common lick in slack key called a turnaround or "vamp", so take the time to get it right. If you are having trouble, take a look at the notes to Example 1 on page 26.

Measure 4: After a gentle strum, play the open fourth string with your thumb, followed by the first string at the 9th fret with your index finger. Note the syncopation, a common theme with slack key. The eighth-note strums are just to fill out the measure, you can leave them off if you want.

Measure 5: Same as measure 1.

Measure 6: Barre everything at the second fret for a D chord, then reach up with your pinky to play the note at fret 5. Again, pay attention to the syncopation!

Measures 7: Play the turnaround figure just as you did in the third measure.

Measure 8: The melody ends back where it started, on the tonic.

Measures 9 & 10: Here's that extra two measure turnaround, a stock feature of Hawaiian songs. By now you should have this lick down!

The C6 chord adds a nice bit of sweetness to round out the arrangement. You can either end here, or go back to the beginning and start over.

'Ukulele Slack Key #1
Basic Version

Low G Taropatch tuning

Mark Kailana Nelson

Performance Notes

'Ukulele Slack Key #1 is my take on a classic type of slack key guitar piece. Every player has their own version–Ray Kāne's *Punahele,* Leonard Kwan's *Manini,* and Ozzie Kotani's *Kani Kī Ho'alu* are just three examples.

Before starting, take a look at the music. Notice that there are three sections, marked A, B and C. Tunes like *'Ukulele Slack Key #1* work by setting up a couple of simple patterns that develop over time through increasingly complex variations. This is the most basic arrangement of the piece, we'll be seeing it in a couple of different settings later on.

Take a look at the staff above the TAB to get an idea of the picking pattern. All of the notes with downward facing stems are played with your thumb, use your fingers for everything else. Notice that the last two measures of each section–a variation of the turnaround we saw in the previous tune–are the same.

Measures 1, 2 & 3: Play the harmonics by lightly touching the strings immediately above the fret. Do not press the string into the fret, just rest your finger gently. You might need to adjust your hand slightly up or down the string before you get a clear tone. Note that the bass note changes in measure 3.

Measures 4 & 5: Play the turnaround using single notes, no need to hold a chord.

Once you can play the whole A section in time and with no mistakes, move on to the next bit.

Measures 6 & 7: The F#–a raised fourth of the tonic chord–is what I call "the Hawaiian Blue Note." It lends a cool, jazzy dissonance to the music. Practice moving quickly from the open string up to the harmonic on the 12th fret. Start moving up when you play the open C string with your thumb.

Measure 8: Same idea, different chord. Notice how the two harmonics complete the G7th chord.

Measures 9 & 10: No surprises here.

Measures 11 & 12: The C section employs an alternating picking pattern between the first and second strings. I move my whole hand up and play the A on fret five with my index finger. Take it slowly until it becomes second nature.

Measure 13: There are a couple of ways to handle the note on the fourth fret; I use my pinky while holding down the second string, first fret with my index finger.

Once you feel comfortable with each section, trying playing them all together. Be sure to take the repeats!

Taropatch Turnarounds & Double Stops

As you learned playing through the previous two songs, slack key makes extensive use of a figure called the turnaround, or vamp. Essentially, the turnaround is a one or two measure lick that moves from a dominant seventh chord back to the tonic—in this case G7 to C.

There are endless variations—in fact, you can often identify individual slack key players just by listening to the way they play the vamp! To really understand the style, it is a good idea to take some time to practice a few common licks.

Example 1: This is the same lick you played in *Kealoha*. The trick is to get a smooth flow between all of the notes, what the Hawaiians call *nahenahe*.

Start this lick by holding a G7 chord fretted on the second and third strings:

Pluck the lowest string with you thumb, then play the third string with your index finger. Sound the open second string and hammer-on to the first fret. Be sure to give each note its full rhythmic value. Then pluck the open first string.

Reach up with your pinky to play the next note on the fourth fret. At this point, you should be holding this chord:

Finally, slide into the note at the fifth fret as you let go of the G7 chord. Let this note ring as you play the open C string with your thumb.

Example 2: Here's a jazzy little gem from the golden age of Waikiki:

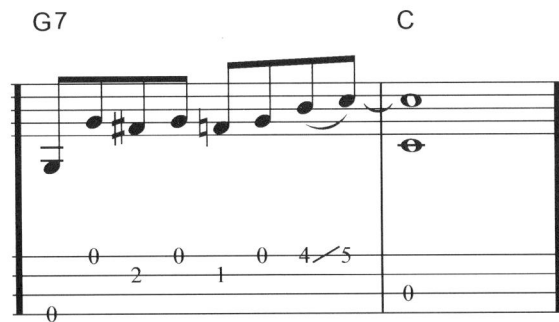

No real tricks here. Play the bass note with your thumb, and then alternate between the first and second strings with one or two fingers on your picking hand. Finish up with the open C string played with your thumb.

Example 3: And now for something really fun!

The trick here is to hold the fretted notes on the second and third strings through the entire first measure. Pluck the open G string with your thumb, then brush upwards with your index finger and immediately execute the rapid triplet slur on the first string.

Play the open G string and the second string as a pinch with your thumb and index fingers.

Finish out the measure and then play the downbeat of the next measure as another pinch.

Double stops—notes played on two strings—are another distinguishing feature of slack key.

Here is a C major scale on the first string harmonized on the third string:

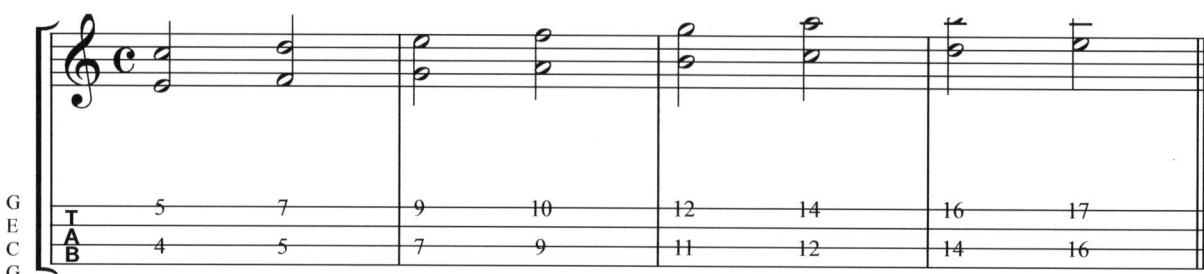

The term "double stop" is actually a bit of a misnomer. Slack key players rarely play the two strings simultaneously, rather they will move through the shapes while employing various picking patterns.

Here are a couple of ways to play ascending and descending scales. Sound the open fourth string with your thumb as you alternate melody notes using your index and middle fingers.

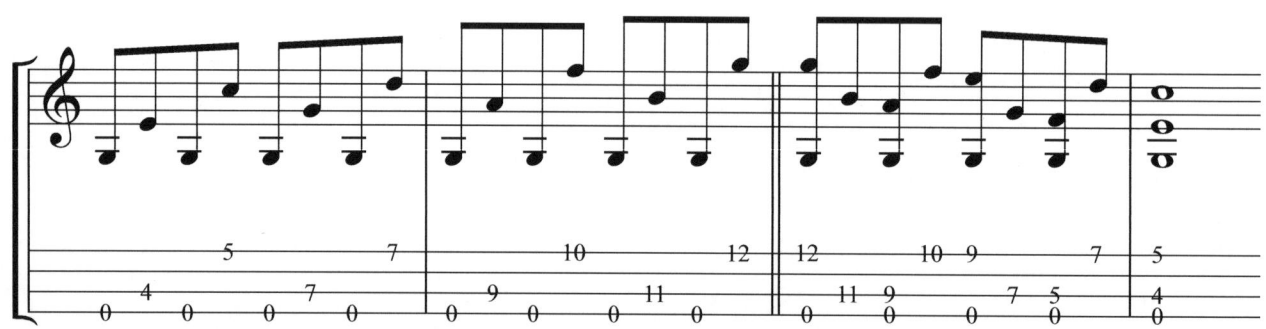

Here are double stops on the first and second strings. I will leave it to you to develop your own exercises.

Finally, take a look at a quintessential Hawaiian turnaround:

It is actually easier than it looks.

The trick is to play out of double stop positions.

The next few arrangements make extensive use of these licks, so be sure you have them under your fingers before you proceed.

Salomila
slack key style

trad

Low G Taropatch

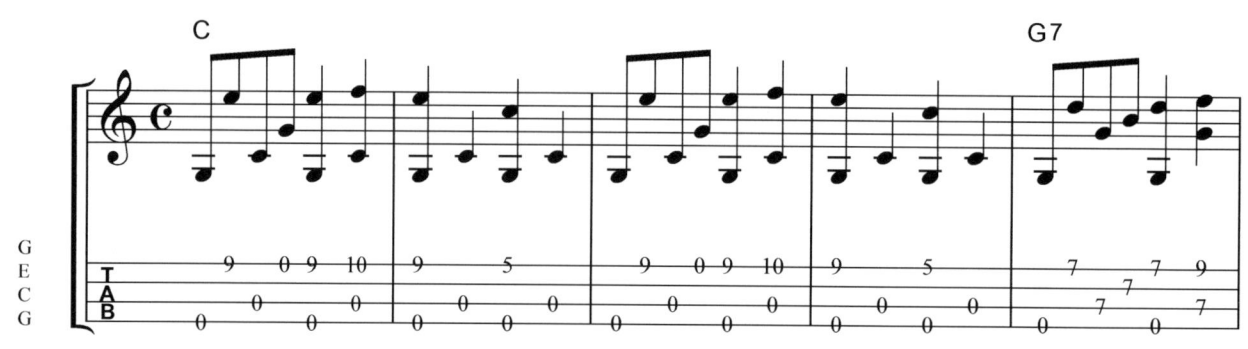
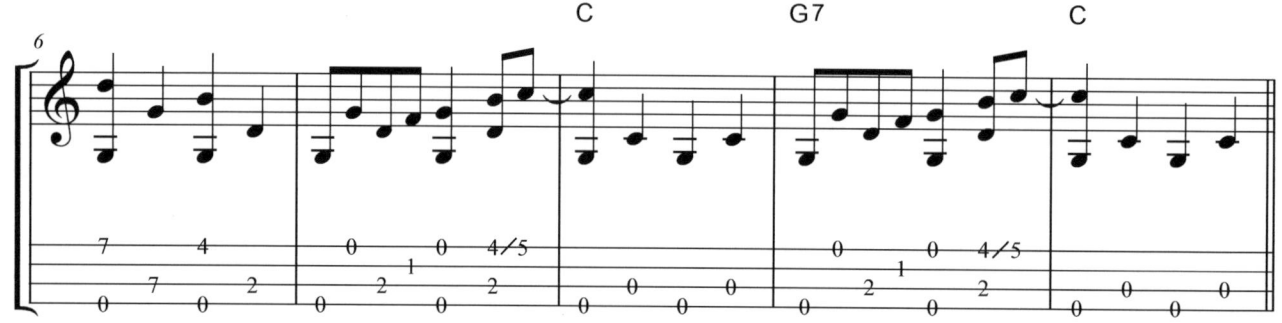

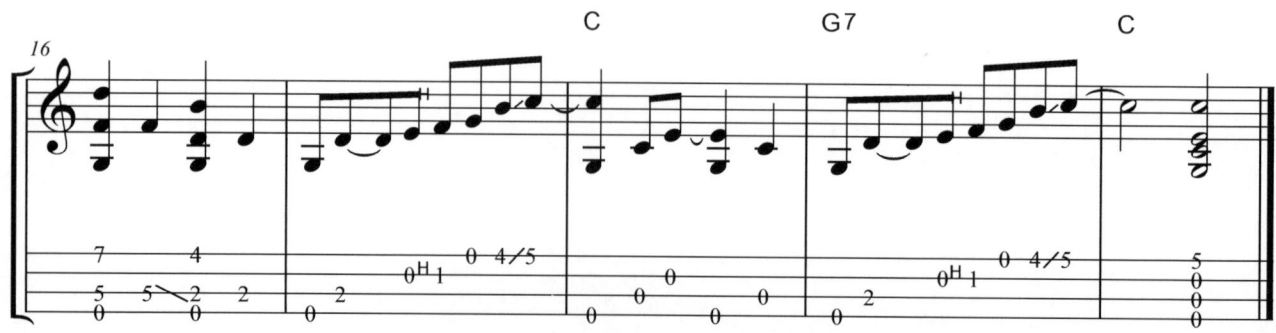

Performance Notes

Salomila tells the tale of a saucy young women who breaks a lot of hearts. Approach the song in a playful manner. The arrangement demonstrates two different approaches to playing in the slack key style.

Measures 1- 4: The first time through, the melody is played as single notes on the first string, with a minimal accompaniment. Notice the alternating bass pattern on the third and fourth strings. Play these notes with your thumb. It may take some time before you are able to hold a steady rhythm.

Measure 5: Hold a partial barre at the seventh fret. Don't forget to keep up the thumb pattern!

Measure 6: Halfway through the measure, move out of the barre to a double stop on frets 2 and 4.

The next four measures ought to feel pretty comfortable by now. You can keep up the alternating bass pattern all the way through.

Measures 11 - 16: For the reprise, the melody changes slightly. The use of slides and harmony in 6ths is typical of the style. If you have been practicing playing double stops, these fingerings should be familiar.

One big difference from the first time through is that the strict alternating bass changes to a half-note pulse played on the open fourth string.

Be sure to look ahead in each measure to determine how to fret the melody notes.

For instance, measure 11 starts with a quick slide up to a double stop at frets 7 & 9 and then moves up to a double stop at 9 and 10. Do not lift your fingers away from the first and third strings at any time during these six measure!

The more you can play out of double stop positions, the more you will be able to smoothly connect the notes.

Papakolea
slack key style

Johnny Almeida

Low G Taropatch

Performance Notes

Here's a lovely melody that really shows off the slack key style.

I play the doubled open strings in the first and fifth measures as gentle upward brushes with my index finger.

Papakolea– which describes a flirtation–makes a great medley with *Kealoha* and the next tune, *Mauna Loa*.

By now you should be fairly familiar with the style, so no more playing notes for the next few arrangements.

Mauna Loa

Helen Lindsey Parker

Low G Taropatch Tuning

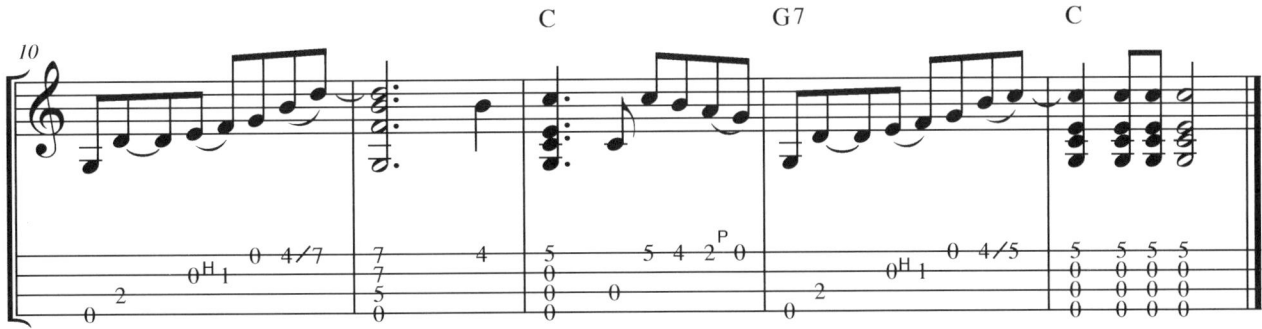

Mauna Loa tells the story of a love affair that has ended.

Ha'ina 'ia mai ana ka puana lā	The story is told
Kū 'oe a hele pēla	Now just get out!
A na'u nō ia 'oni ho'okahi lā	It is not my lot to be alone and restless
E ---- e ---- e	E --- e ---e
I kahi pela a'o kāua	Where we two used to be

© 2010 Acme Arts. All Rights Reserved

Aloha ʻOe

Queen Liliʻuokalani

Low G Taropatch Tuning

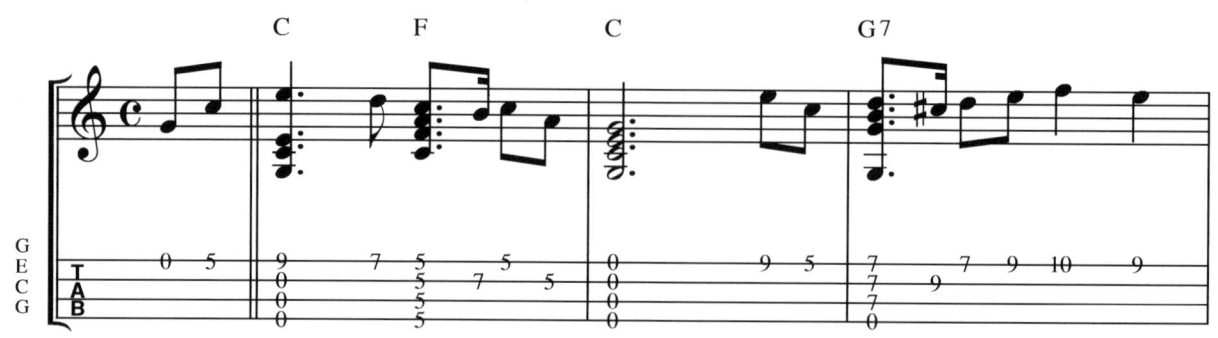

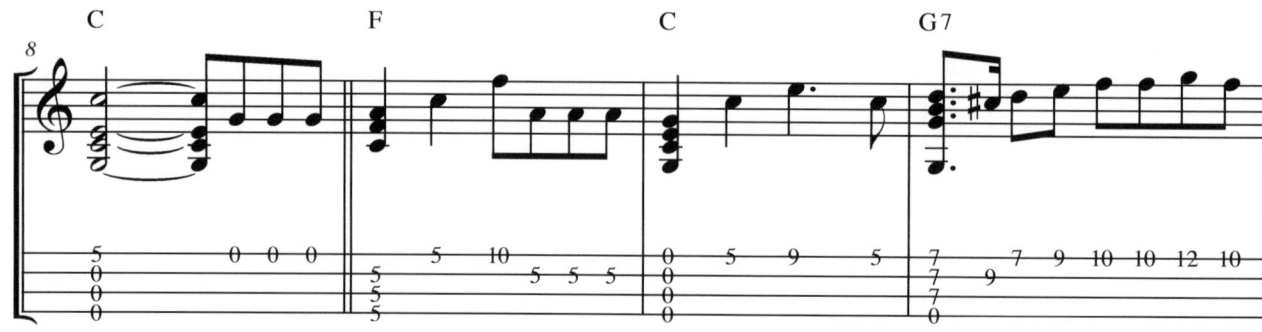

One of the most recognizable melodies in the world, the Queen's song of parting has become a symbol of Hawai'i.

Play this with a stately grace.

Ahe Lau Makani
slack key version

Queen Liliʻuokalani

Low G Taro Patch

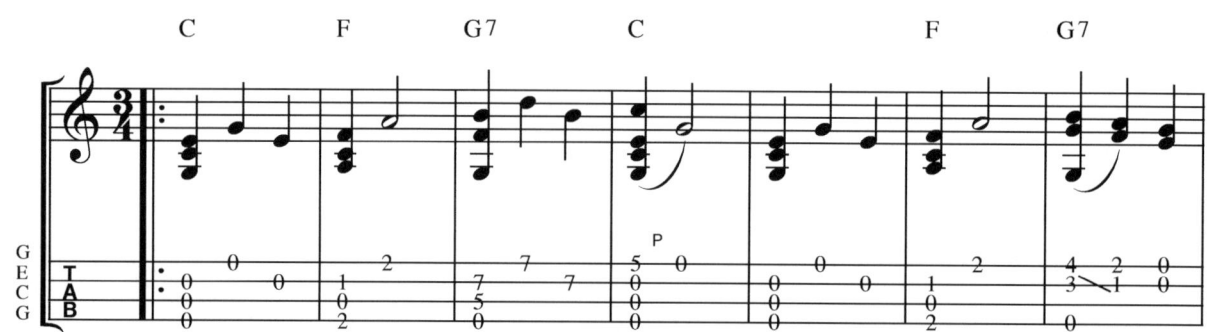
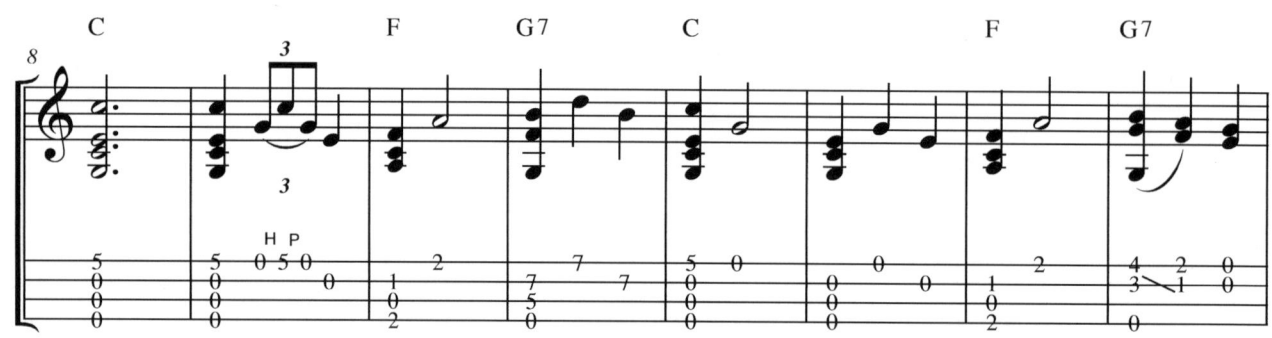
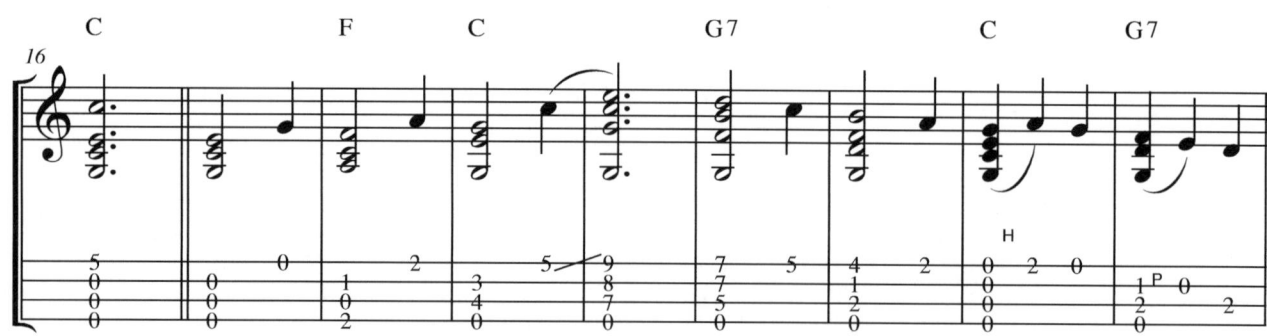

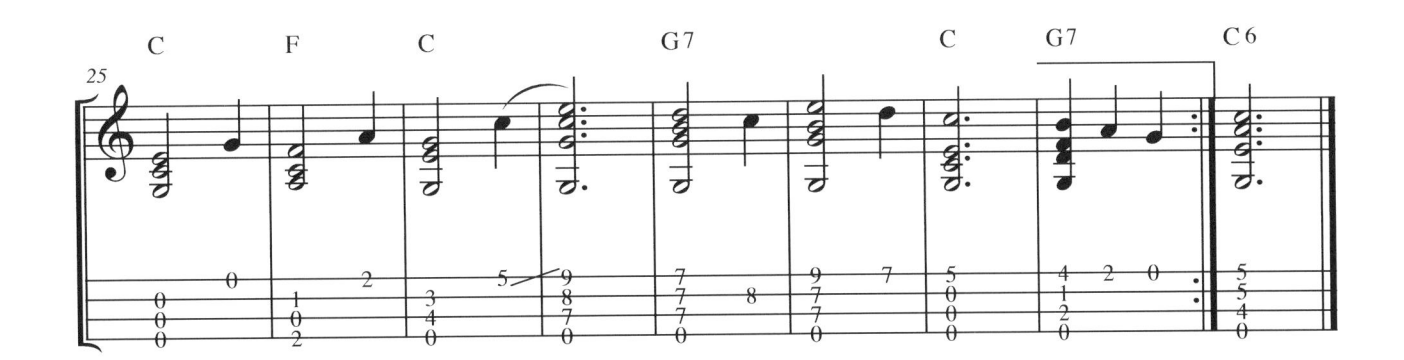

Performance Notes

Here's another look at a song you played at the beginning of the book to help you see how a slack key player might approach creating an arrangement. Later on, you'll get to play another version.

The arrangement is fairly self-explanatory, but take a few moments to look it over before you dive in. Notice the use of slurs, like the long pull-off from the fifth fret to the open string in measure 4, or the double stop slides in measures 7 and 15.

Measures 1 - 3: This arrangement will work equally well using partial strums or played fingerstyle. I generally set it up with my thumb on the fourth string, and one finger per string; employing a very quick roll for each of the chords.

Measure 9: I play the hammer-on with my pinky to set up the F chord in the next measure; use whatever finger works best.

Measures 19 & 20: Play the long slide from the fifth fret to the ninth, and then pick the note again when you play the chord on the downbeat.

Measure 32: This is the first ending, from here go back to the top of the song. Try to find subtle ways to vary you playing the second time through. Then skip this measure and jump to the chord in measure 33.

'Ukulele Slack Key #1
Version 2

Low G Taropatch tuning

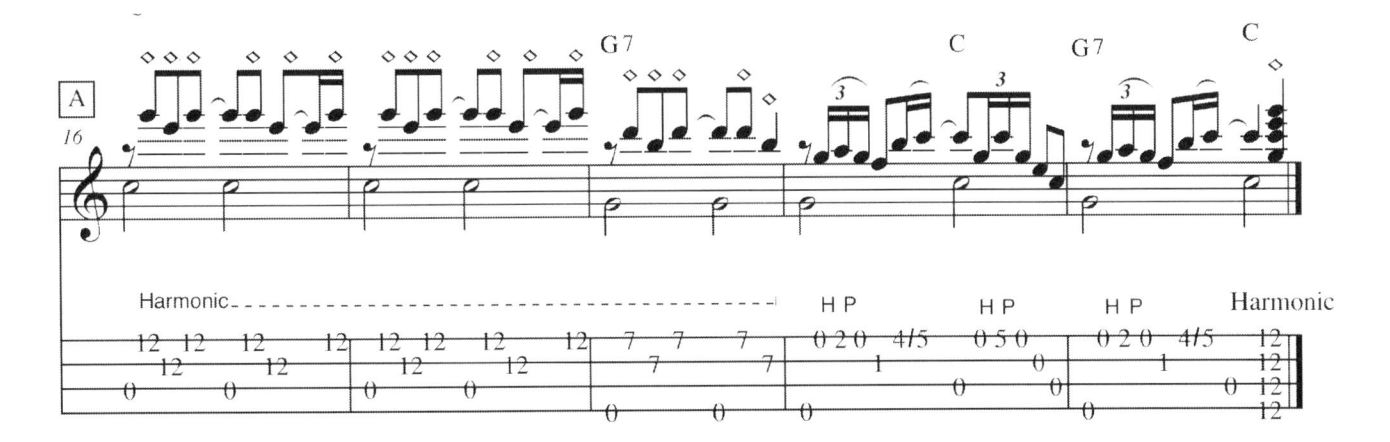

Performance Notes

For this version of the song, I have added a bit more complexity to each section. The syncopation, triplet slurs and slides are all typical of the slack key style.

Compare this to the basic version on page 24.

Measures 1 & 2: Notice how the extra sixteenth note at the end of each measure kicks you into the next downbeat.

Measures 4 & 5: Same general idea; this time sliding into the tonic just ahead of the downbeat.

Measures 6 & 7: Play the triplet as a rapid hammer-on/pull-off combination. It is your choice whether or not to hold the F# on the second string while playing the slurs. Sometimes I do, sometimes I don't.

Measure 8: Same basic idea.

Measures 9 & 10: Even the turnaround gets the triplets!

Measures 11 & 12: I play the slurs around the second fret with my index finger and use my pinky for the fifth fret. If you have trouble flicking your pinky for the rapid hammer-on/pull-off combination, feel free to use a different fingering.

Measure 13: Try to hold the F on the first fret, second string for this entire measure.

Measures 16 - 20: A reprise of the A section to end the tune.

After you are comfortable playing these variations, add them to the original version to create a longer arrangement.

Changing Keys in Taropatch Tuning

Up until now, all of the songs have been in the key of C, because Taropatch tuning contains a C major triad. But how do you play in other keys?

Slack key guitarists often make use of related tunings; for instance, simply by changing the lowest string from a D to a C a guitarist can move from Taropatch to Leonard Kwan's "Drop C" tuning. As an 'ukulele player, you have it even easier—the top four strings in Taropatch and Drop C are identical, so there is nothing to retune!

The next couple of arrangements move to the key of F. Familiarize yourself with this chord shape; it will be your home position in this key.

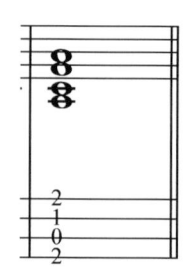

Notice that, by moving to the key of F, the open strings now outline the dominant chord, and the open E string is the seventh tone of the F major scale. In fact, that major seventh interval is so important that Hawaiian call such tunings *wahine* tunings, for the Hawaiian word for woman.

Why? Well, I have heard a lot of stories, but maybe it is just because *wahine* tunings sound so sweet!

Here are some double stops on the second and fourth strings.

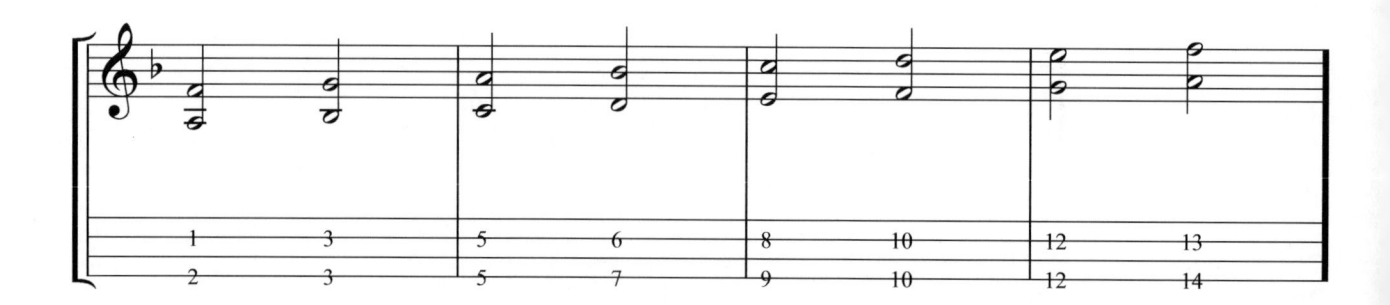

A hammer-on back to the tonic is the characteristic sound of *wahine* tunings, as you can hear in the next two turnarounds.

Example 1: Notice the syncopation; the lick starts after the downbeat. I play the notes on the fourth string with my thumb. You can either hammer-on or slide from the second to the third fret; but whichever you choose, strive for a smooth connection between all of the notes.

After the hammer-on, hold the note on the third fret so it continues to ring while you play the two open strings. You want to be able to clearly hear the C7 chord. Let go of the chord as you hammer-on to the first fret.

Although it is not notated, I place the F chord almost simultaneously with the hammer-on.

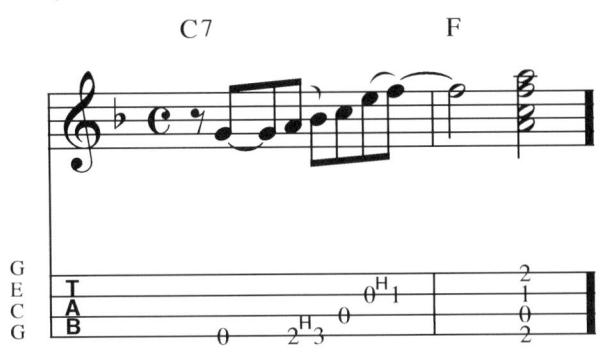

Example 2: Same idea, different sound. Try for the sound of water falling down a mountain stream.

Example 3: And here is the classic Hawaiian vamp. Remember to play out of the double stop positions!

Pūpū Hinuhinu

Slack Key Style

Nona Beamer

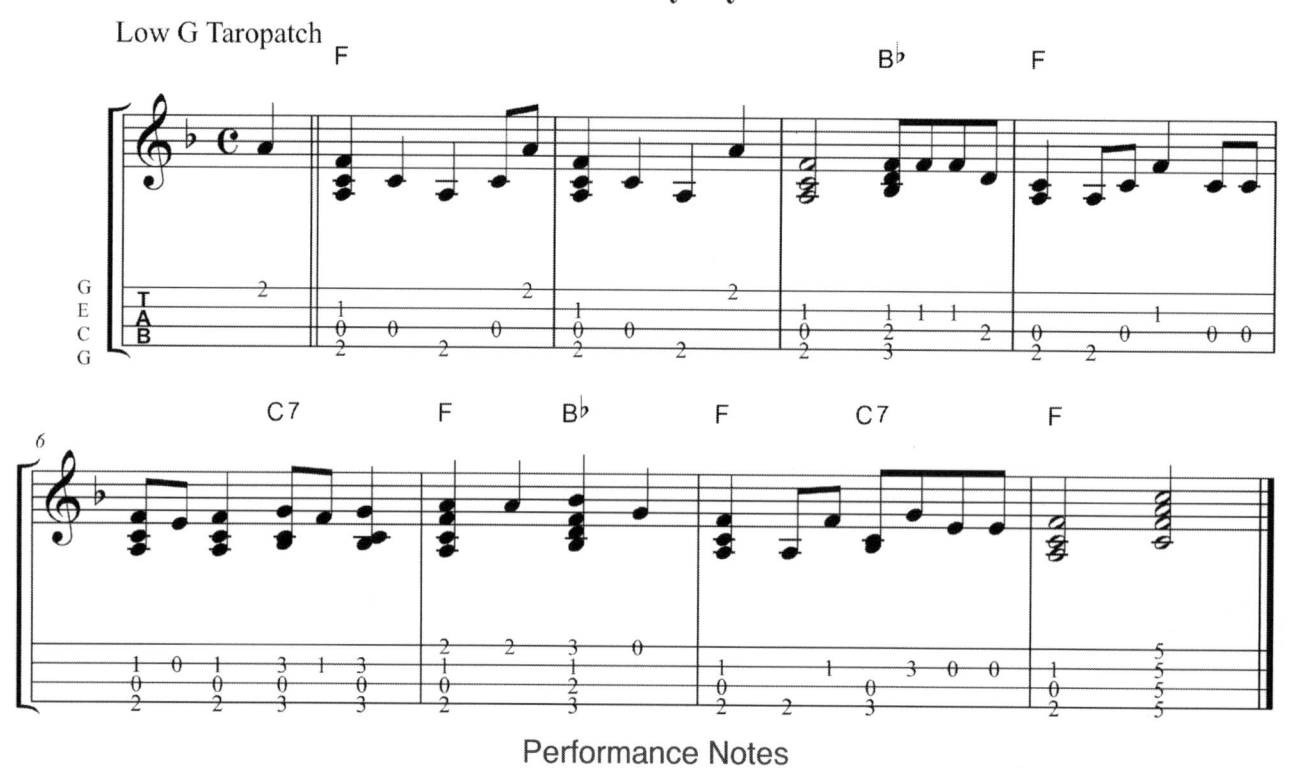

Low G Taropatch

Performance Notes

Other than introducing some unfamiliar chord shapes, this arrangement should not pose a challenge. Compare it to the first song in the book.

Measures 1-3: Set up the F chord for the pick-up and hold it until the next chord change. I have added some addition notes to add support to the melody.

At measure three, grab a B♭ chord on the bottom three strings. Yep, it is exactly the same fingering as in standard tuning–be careful you don't add a note on the first fret of the first string!

Measure 4: One hallmark of playing in the key of F is that melody notes often fall on the lower strings. Rather that play a full chord, which would confuse the ear, you often play only one or two strings.

Measure 7: Notice that the four-string B♭ chord has a different shape from the grip used in standard tuning. Once you get used to the idea that you have to shift notes two frets higher to compensate for the lowered first string, you will be able to quickly adapt chord shapes you already know.

© 2010 Acme Arts. All Rights Reserved

Kowali
slack key style

Johnny Almeida

Low G Taropatch

Performance Notes

The *Kowali* (sometimes spelled *koali*) is a pretty flower of the Morning Glory familiy whose blossoms brighten many Hawaiian beaches.

Measure 2: The melody falls out of a B♭ chord, but I chose to play them as single notes.

Measure 3: It is harder to keep a steady bass pattern when playing in the key of F. Notice how the next few measures suggest an alternating bass on the lowest two strings.

Measures 7 & 9: This is a variation of turnaround Example 1 on page 41.

© 2010 Acme Arts. All Rights Reserved

He Aloha Noʻo Honolulu

Lot Kauwe

Low G Taropatch

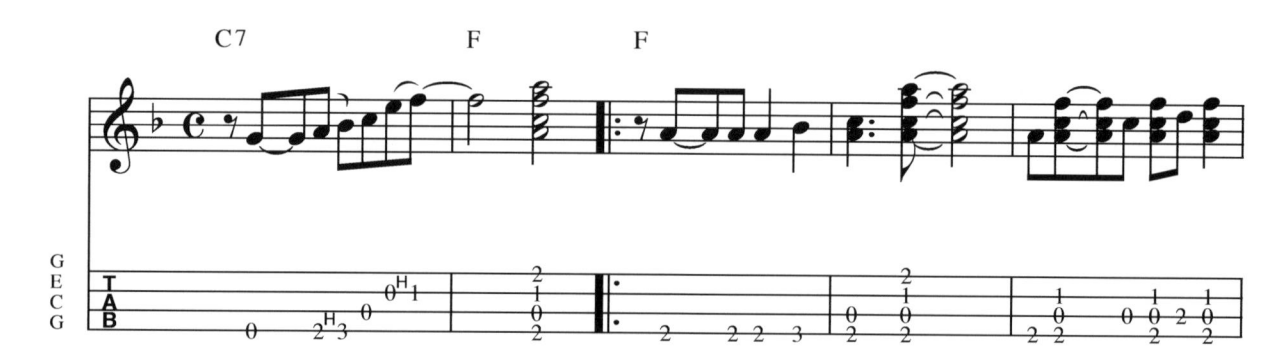

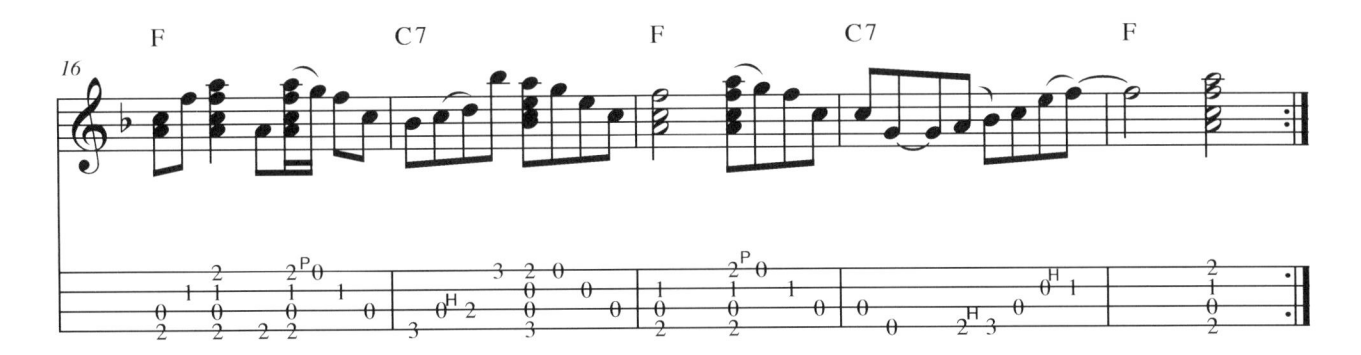

Performance Notes

On the surface, this song is about sailing from Honolulu to the district of Kona on the Big Island. Ah, but is it really about a love affair?

Measures 1 & 2: Just a little turnaround to set up the melody. It is common for slack key players to play a short introduction to prepare the listener for what is to come. If you are playing in a *kanikapila*–jam session–an introductory turnaround or two helps everyone find the correct tempo.

Measure 3: This is the beginning of the song. Any harmony on the upper strings would mask the melody. I generally take this song at a pretty good clip, so the four beats of unadorned single notes go by quickly.

Measure 6: The melody is pretty sparse and syncopated here, so I have added a couple of strums at the end of the measure to fill things out. Try not to strum too loudly; just give a quick up and down brush. You will see variations on this idea throughout the rest of the song.

Measure 9: Hold a partial B♭ chord for this measure.

Measures 11 & 12: A variation of the first two measures of the song.

Measure 16: Things are starting to get interesting! Do not let go of the F chord until the downbeat of the next measure.

Measure 17: I hold the fourth string at the third fret for this whole measure. The second chord is a C9–sweet!.

Hiʻilawe

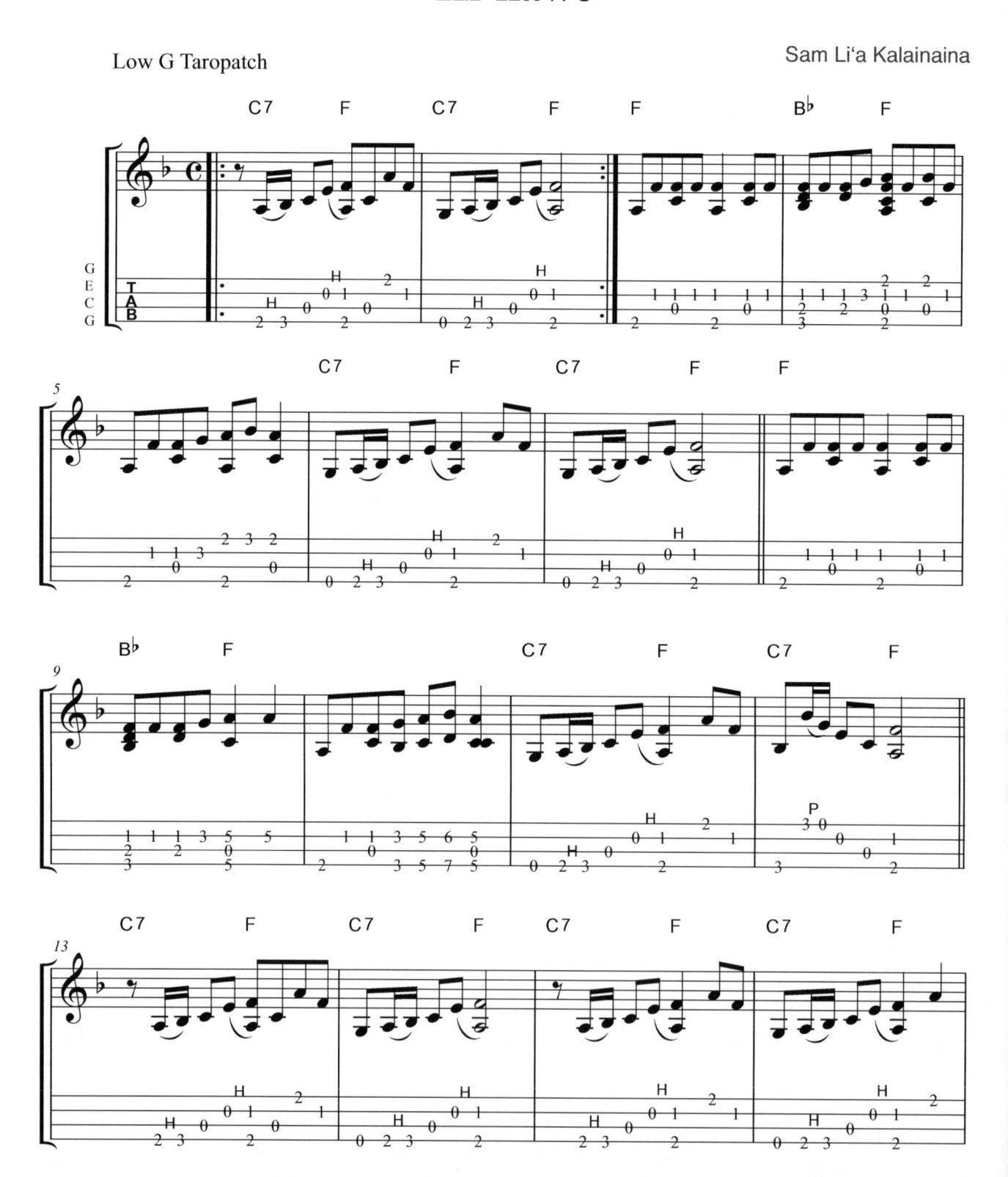

Low G Taropatch

Sam Liʻa Kalainaina

47

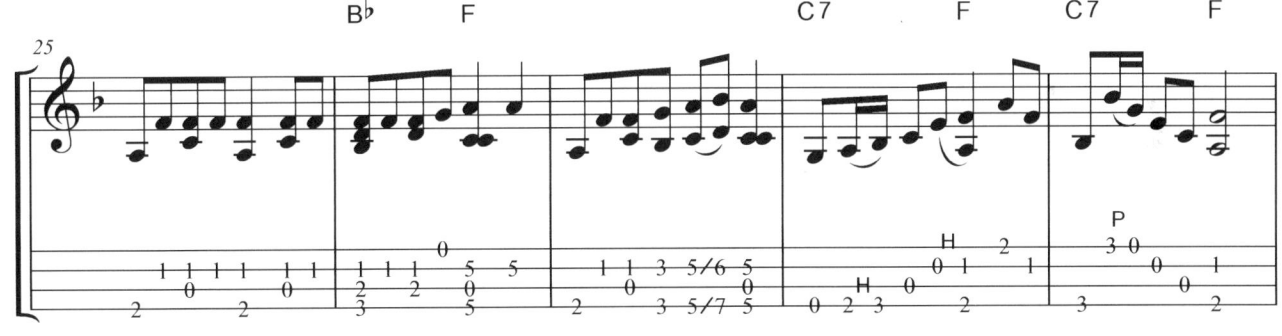

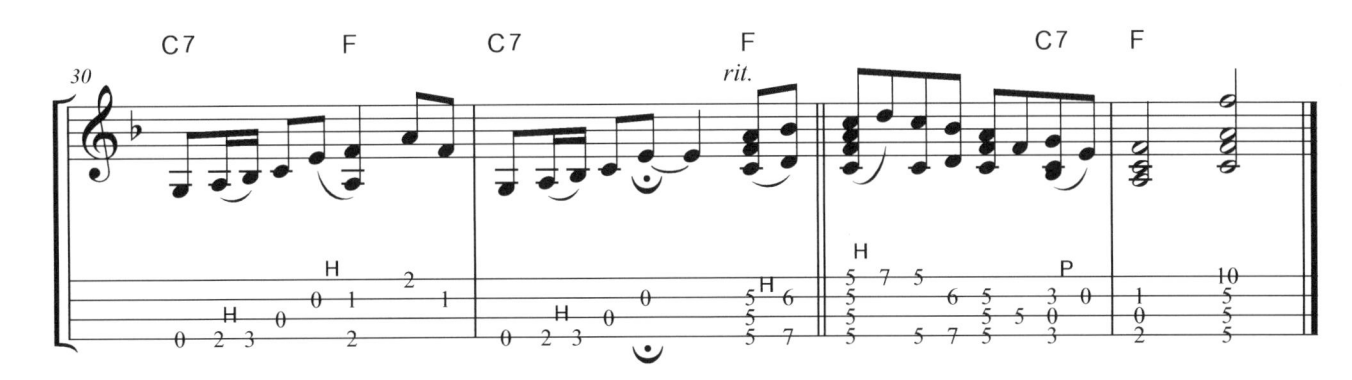

Hiʻilawe Performance Notes

You cannot play slack key without playing *Hiʻilawe*! This classic song about an illicit love affair near the twin waterfalls at the head of Waipiʻo Valley was the first Hawaiian slack key song ever recorded.

Measures 1 & 2: The sound of this turnaround is all you need to let listeners know they are in store for some classic, old-style slack key.

Measures 3 - 5: The verse form of the song is quite simple, consisting a single pair of lyrics over four bars. As with many slack key style songs, the final measure of the verse is sung over a turnaround figure.

Kūmaka ka ʻikena iā Hiʻilawe	All eyes are on Hiʻilawe
Ka papa lohi mai aʻo Maukele	In the sparkling lowlands of Maukele

Measures 8 - 11: Just a variation of the same melody, this time adding double stops.

Pakele mai au i ka nui manu	I have not been trapped by the gossip of many birds
Hau wala`au nei puni Waipi`o	Chattering everywhere in Waipiʻo

Measure 12: A variation of the classic *Hiʻilawe* turnaround.

Measure 13: Unless accompanying dancers, singers will typically add an instrumental solo after singing a few verses. The next section is one such instrumental interlude. Notice that it does not follow the chord progression—or even the form—of the verses.

The multitude of slurs and the subtle variations of a basic pattern are all typical of slack key songs in this style. After you have played through measures 13 - 19, try to come up with a few twists of your own.

Measure 19-29: The next two sections reprise the original statements of the melody. Notice how adding slurs or varying the turnaround figure is enough to keep your interest.

Measures 30 - 33: I use a couple of turnarounds to set up a simple coda for the arrangement. In measure 31, hold the note with the fermata for a little longer—just enough to let it breathe. Then grab a barre at the fifth fret and quickly hammer-on both strings. Gradually slow down as you play the next measure and finish up with a pair of chord inversions.

C Wahine Tuning

The next pair of arrangements introduce two new slack key tunings.

The *C Wahine* tuning used in *Paniolo Slack Key* is based on a common slack key guitar tuning sometimes called "Double Slack." It is one of those tunings that is immediately recognizable–songs played in this tuning have that "Real Old Style" sound.

To retune, simply drop the third string one half step, from C to B. Starting on the fourth string, your pitches will now be G - B - E - G.

Like all *wahine* tunings, there is a major seventh interval, in this case between the open B and the tonic note of C on the first fret.

First off, here are the chord positions for the tonic and dominant seventh chords. Yep, one finger. Doesn't get much easier than that, does it?

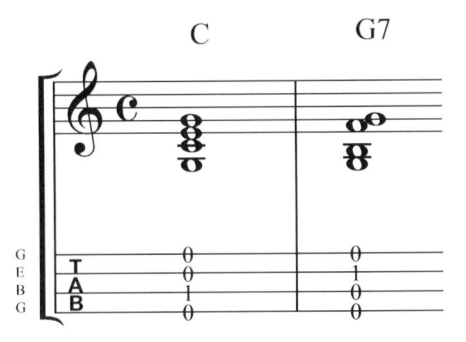

Turnarounds almost always use a hammer-on to move back to the tonic. Practice this two measure riff until it becomes second nature. I use my thumb on the lowest string and my fingers for everything else.

After you play through *Paniolo Slack Key*, I'll show you how to play slack key 'ukulele in standard uke tuning!

Paniolo Slack Key

C Wahine, Low G

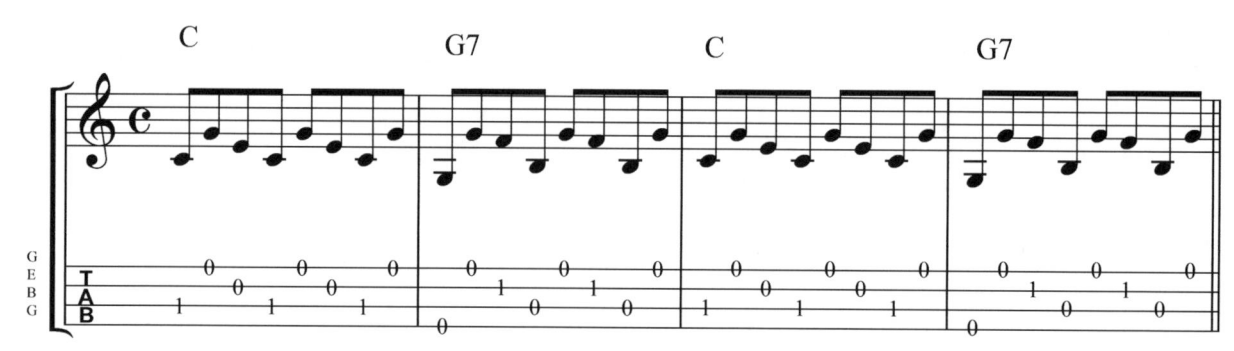

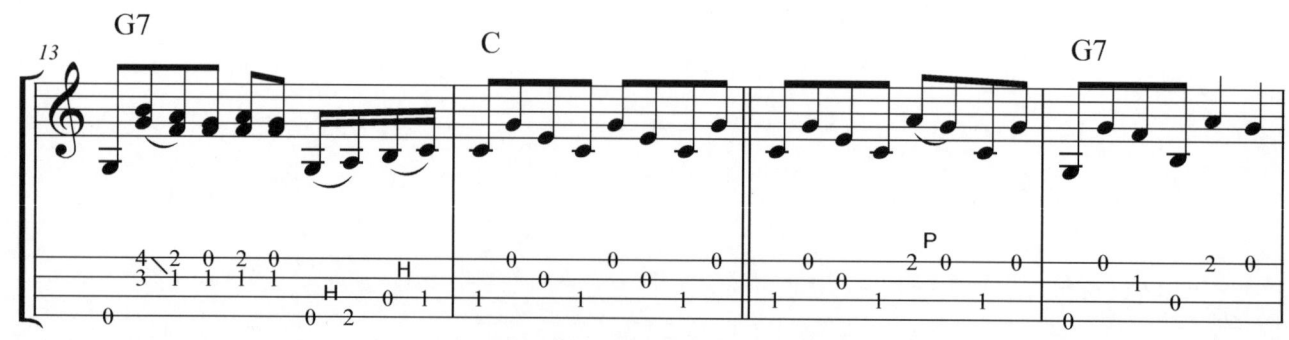

Traditional

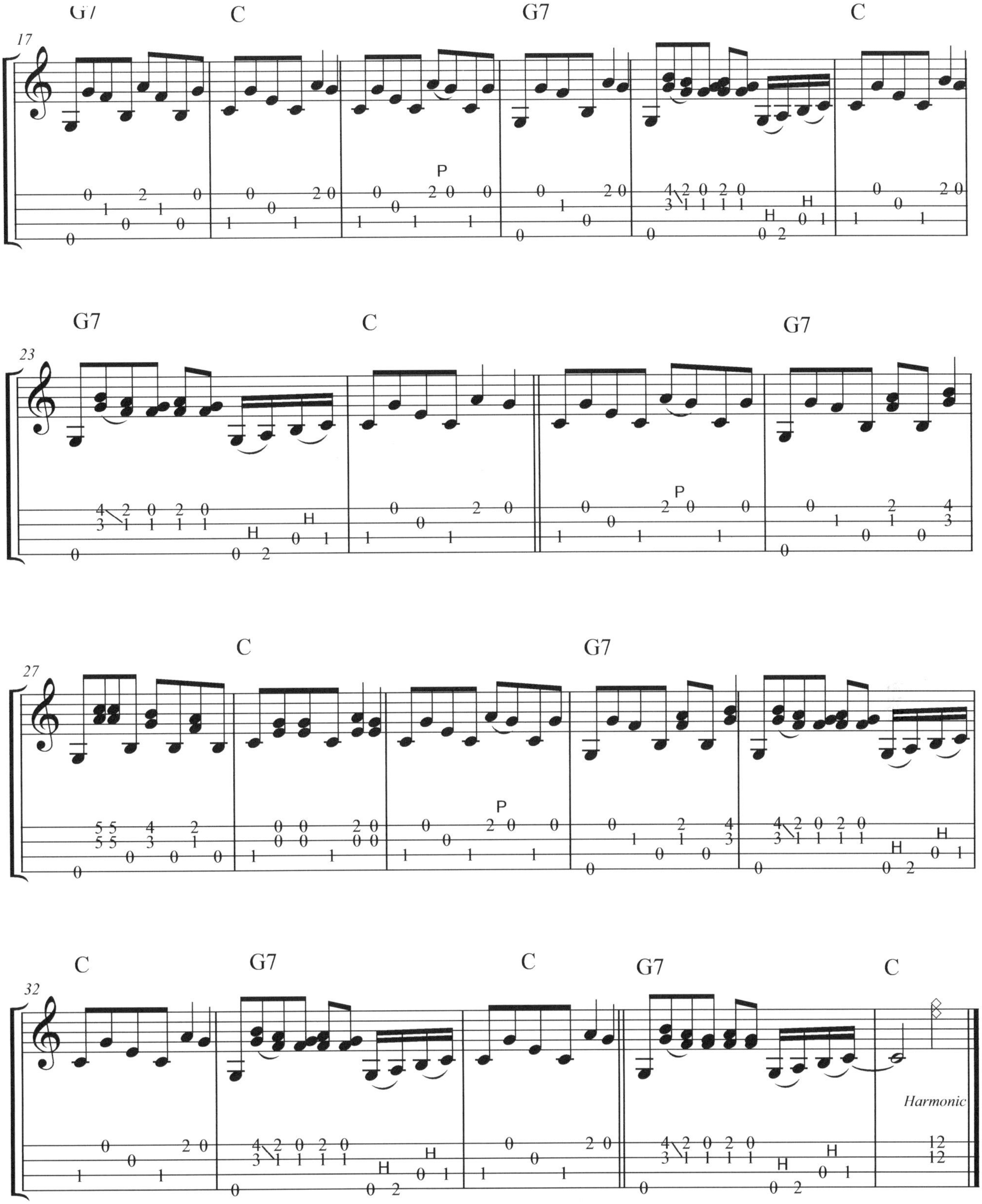
G7
C
G7
C
G7
C
G7
C
G7
C
G7
C
G7
C
Harmonic

Performance Notes

Paniolo Slack Key takes its title from the Hawaiian cowboys who first began playing slack key back in the early ranching days. Pay attention to the Latin-inflections, like the lilting rhythm and the parallel third harmonies.

Measures 1 - 4: The introduction is designed to get your thumb used to playing a syncopated pattern based on the *clave*, an Afro-American rhythm.

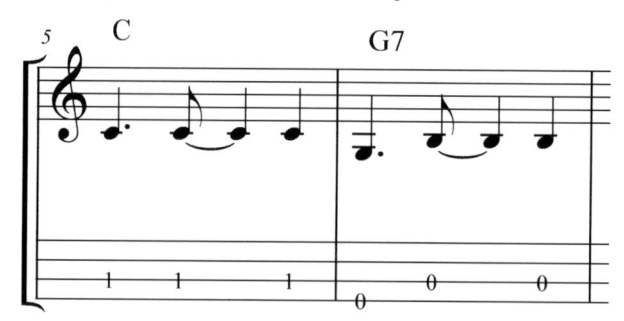

Use your thumb for the third and fourth strings and fingers for the first two strings. The bass pattern will continue for most of the arrangement, so take time to get it right.

Measures 5 - 10: I play the double stops on the first two strings with an upward brush of my index finger.

Measures 11 & 13: This turnaround repeats throughout the arrangement. Play the double stops as before. Alternate between your thumb on the fourth string and index finger on the third for the sixteenth note figure starting on beat three.

Measure 17 From here on, the tune is just a series of slight variations to the original theme. Notice how very simple changes in rhythm, accent or melody can sound new and refreshing.

Measure 18: The bass pattern changes here to add a little space.

Measures 25 - 34: Another slight variation of the melody. After you have played through the whole song a few times, try to find some variations of your own.

Playing "Slack Key Style" in Standard 'Ukulele Tuning

Believe it or not, the standard uke tuning of G-C-E-A is a great tuning for slack key. If you play all four open strings you get a C6th chord.

Adapting slack key stylings to standard tuning lets you move out of the keys of C or F.

Because you will not have as many open strings to work with, it becomes important to play out of chord shapes more often. Different keys lend themselves to different types of double stop licks, too.

Here are some double stops in the key of A:

```
E|-0--2--4--5--|-7--9--11-12-|
B|-1--2--4--6--|-8--9--11-13-|
```

The key of G works great with double stops on the first two strings:

```
E|-2--3--5--7--|-9--10-12-14-|
B|-3--5--7--8--|-10-12-14-15-|
```

Of course, you can play slack key style double stops in the keys of C and F:

```
E|-3--5--7--8--|-10-12-14-15-|
B|-4--5--7--9--|-11-12-14-16-|
```

```
E|-1--3--5--6--|-8--10-12-13-|
B|-2--3--5--7--|-9--10-12-14-|
```

Iesu Me Ke Kanaka Waiwai
"Slack Key" Style

Low G, standard tuning

John K. Almeida

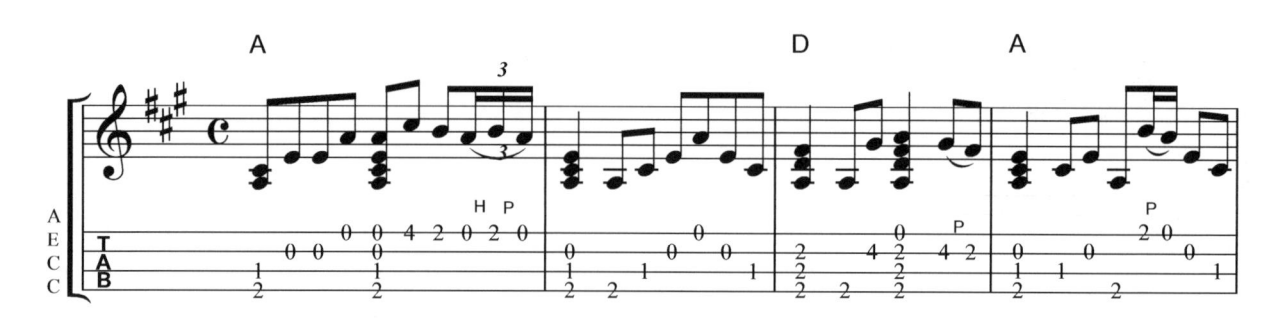

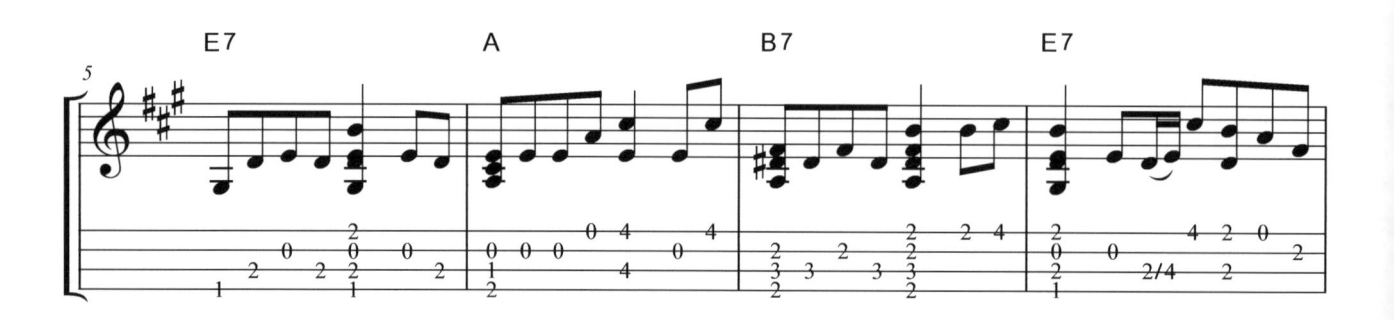

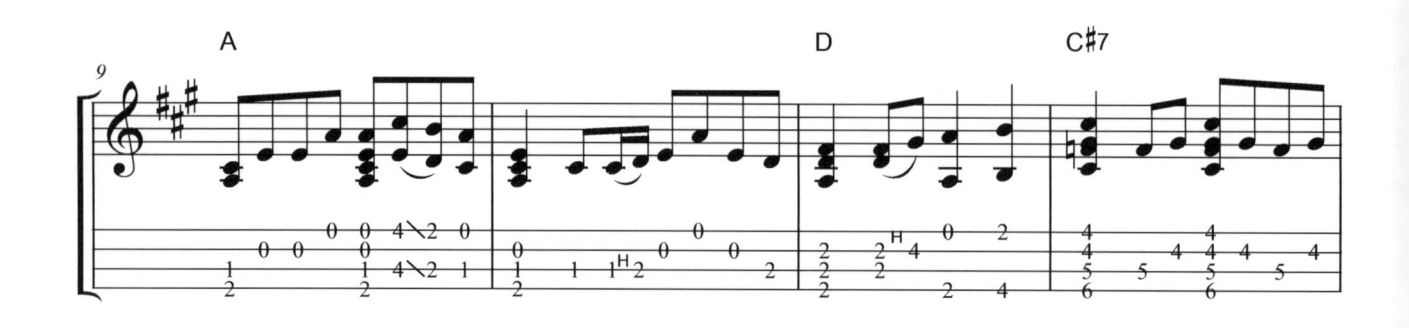

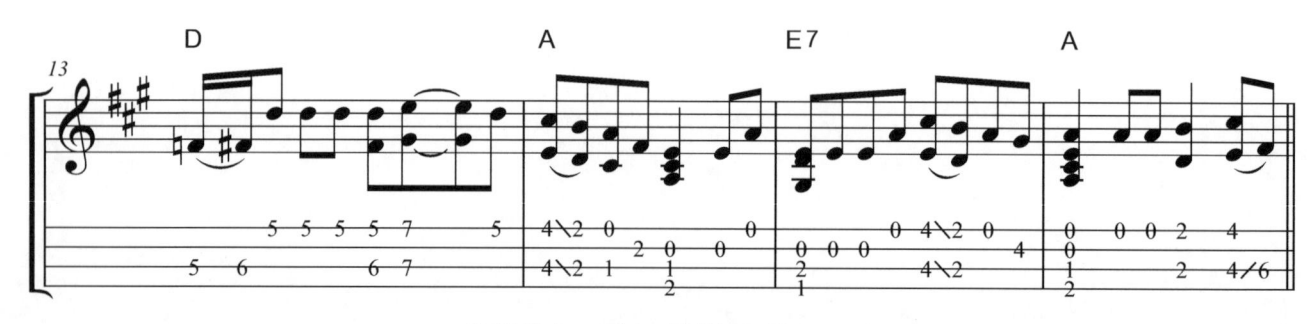

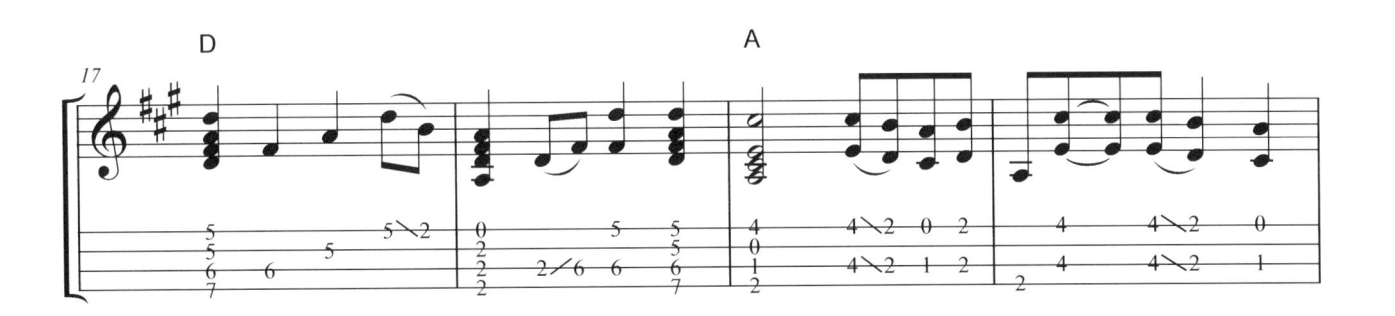

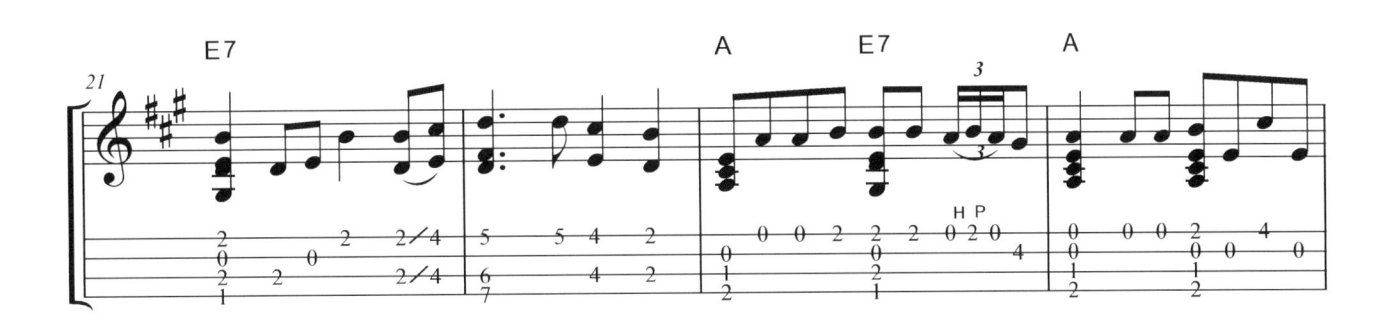

Iesu Me Ke Kanaka Waiwai

Perfomance Notes

Here is another look at *Iesu Me Ke Kanaka Waiwai* in the key of A to illustrate how to apply slack key style licks in standard tuning. Compare this to the basic arrangement on page 18.

Notice I have added the slurs, triplets and double stops similar to those you have played in open tuned arrangements.

Measure 1: Play this entire measure while holding down the A chord. Although you can play any of the chords with a strum, you will achieve a more pleasing effect with a quick roll of your thumb and fingers. The triplet figure at the end of the measure gives the flavor of slack key; you will encounter several variations of this idea in later measures.

Measures 8 & 9: The slides and double stops are characteristic of the slack key style. By now you should be familiar with how to play these.

Measures 10 & 11: Offsetting the melody slightly via a quick hammer-on is another typical trick.

Measure 11: You are actually playing a major chord, not the C#7 written above the staff. Why? Because it completes the ascending bass line started in the previous measure.

Measures 17 & 18: The long slide in measure 17 gets you down to the inversion at the top of the next measure. Then move back up via double stops. You could play the melody out of the higher chord shape, but then you would not be able to add the slurs.

Measure 26: Another use of double stops. Notice that the harmony changes to the dominant chord briefly before moving back to the tonic in the following measure.

Measures 29 - 32: If you are only going to play through this the one time, gradually slow down to bring the song to a restful conclusion.

Later on in the book, I'll give you yet another way to play this beautiful song.

Section Three: Advanced Slack Key Style Arrangements

This last section of the book contains a grab bag of arrangements designed to further your enjoyment and understanding of playing slack key style 'ukulele. Some may pose a challenge, some not.

I offer notes and comments from time to time to explain why I did what I did or how to finger a particularly tricky passage. Remember, if you see a lick or arranging idea you like, go back and add it to a song you have already learned. Experimentation and refinement is the key to developing a personal style.

My goal is to help you develop a solid repertoire of classic melodies.

Have fun, and remember "Jus' Press!"

Moana Chimes

M.K. Moke

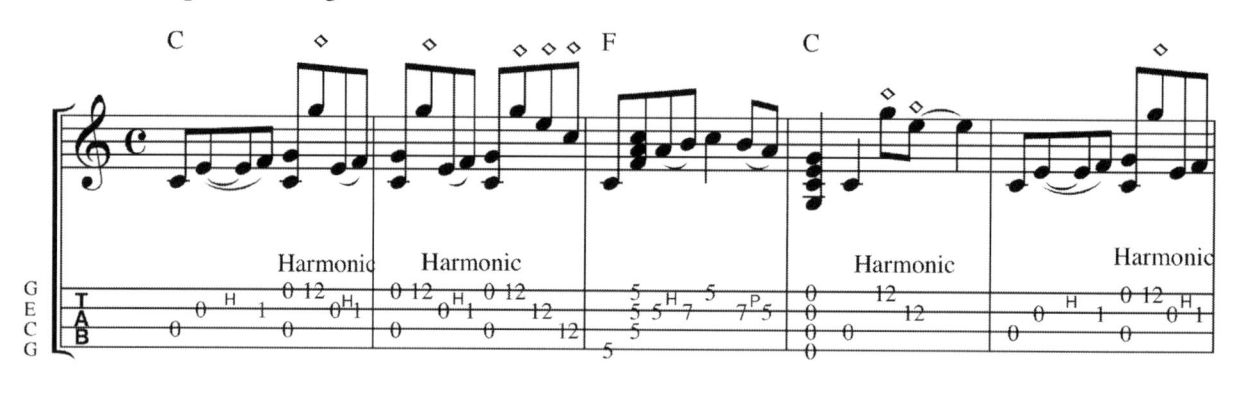

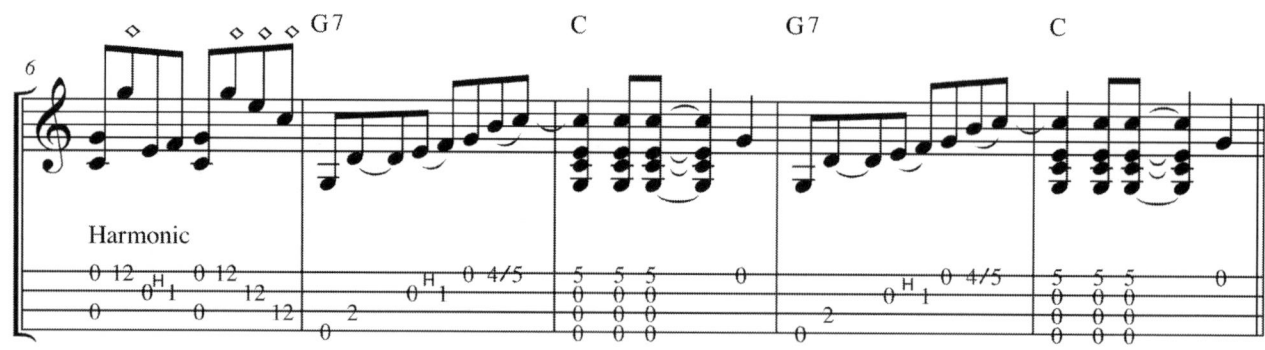

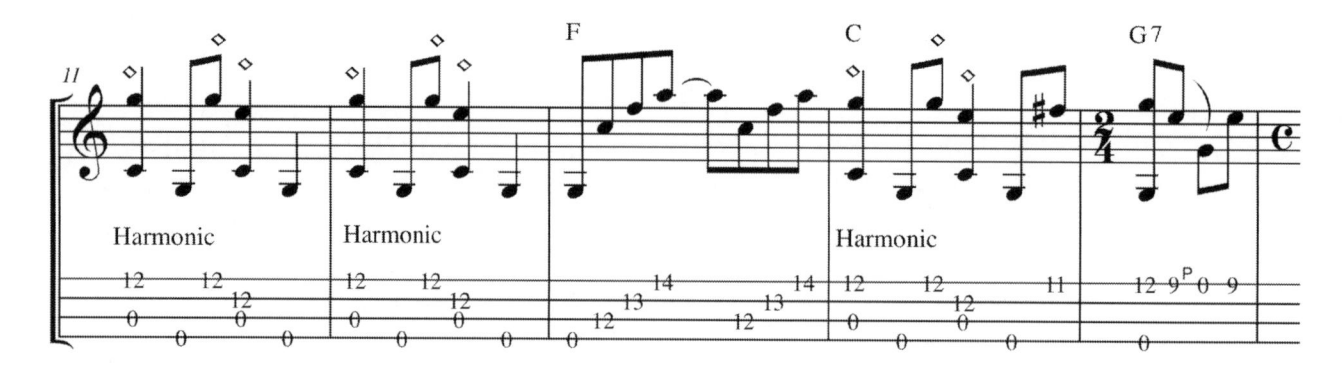

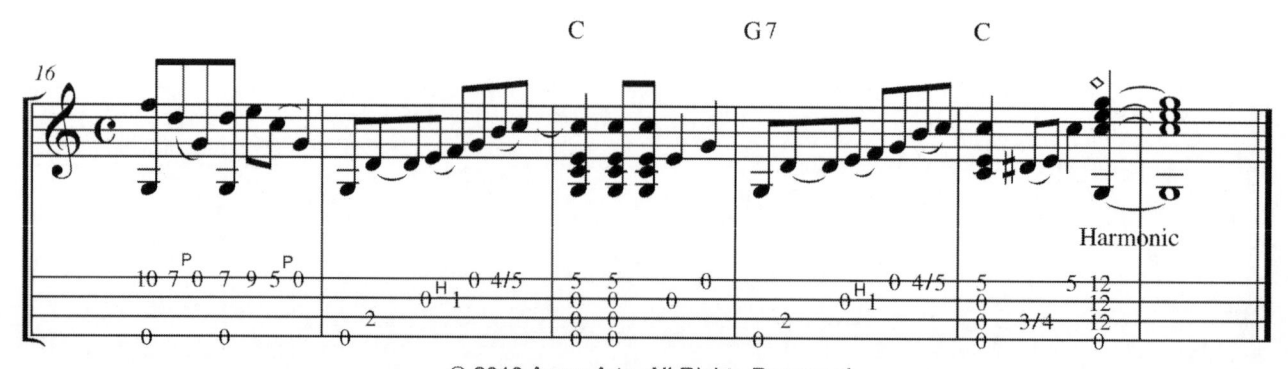

Low G Taropatch Tuning

Kimo's Slack Key
slack key style

trad

Low G Taropatch

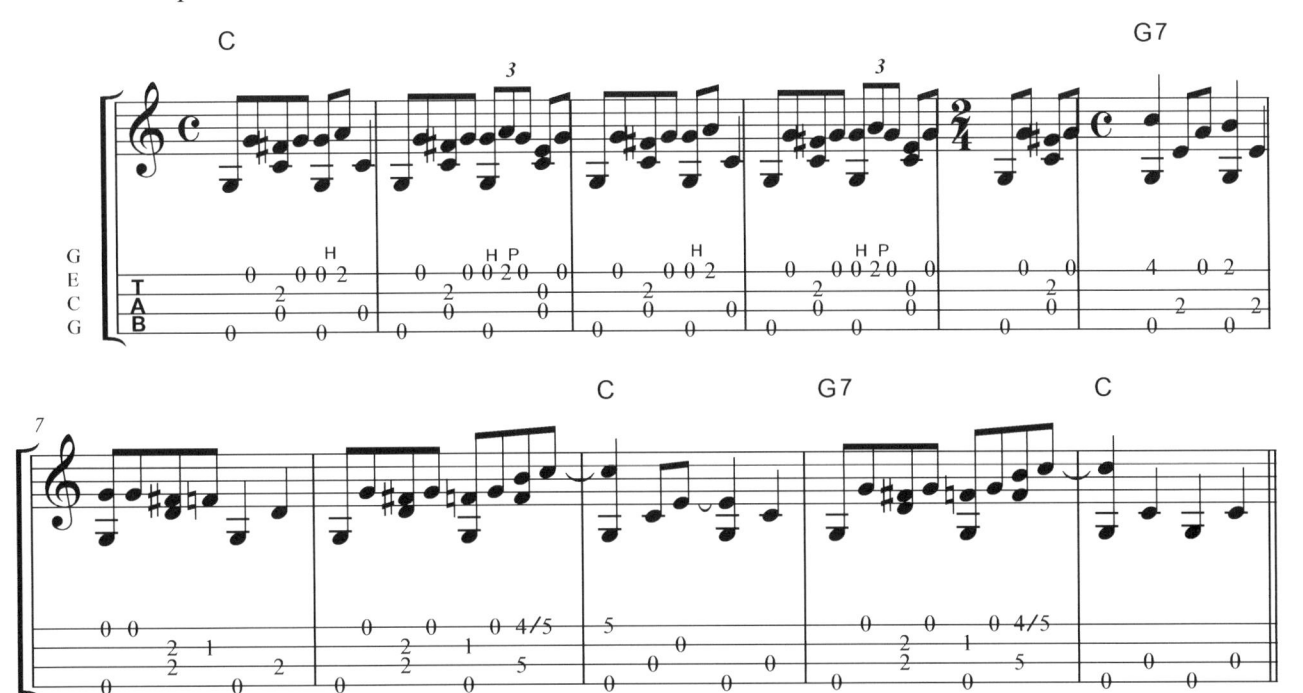

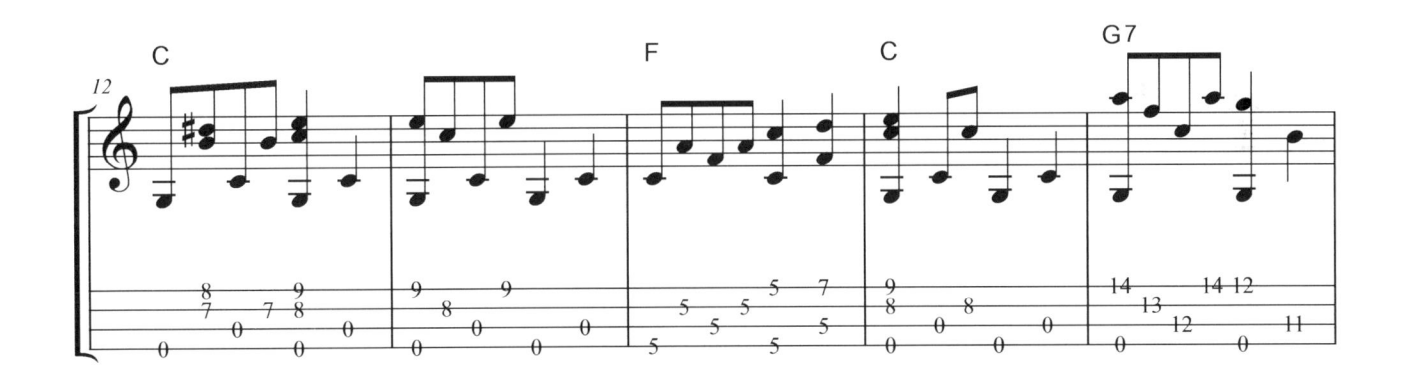

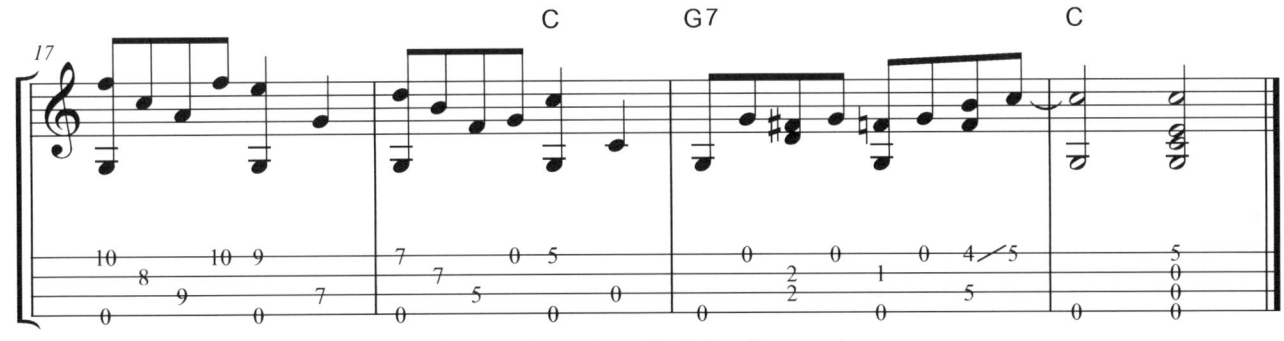

Hula Blues
slack key style

Sonny Cunha

Taropatch tuning

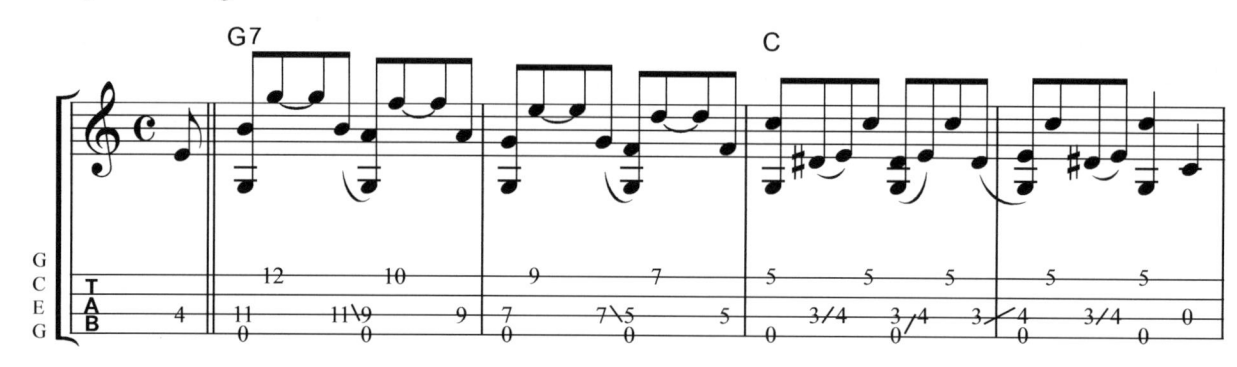

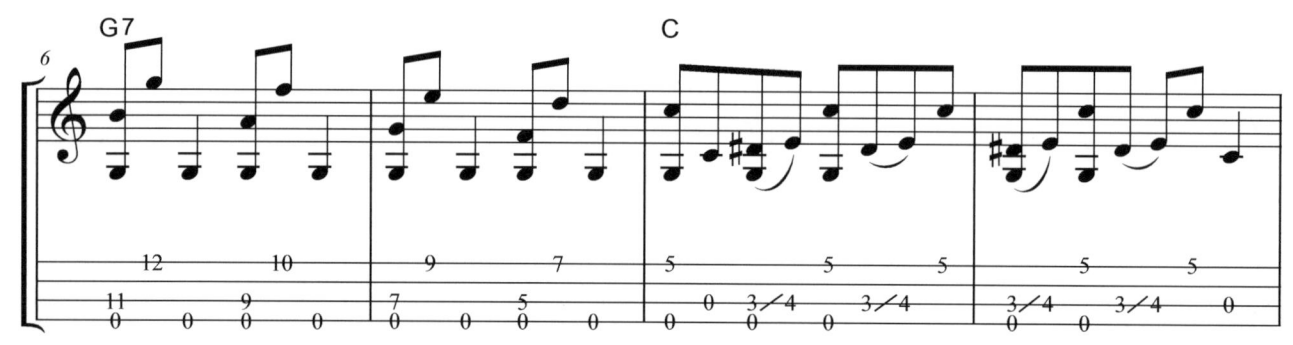

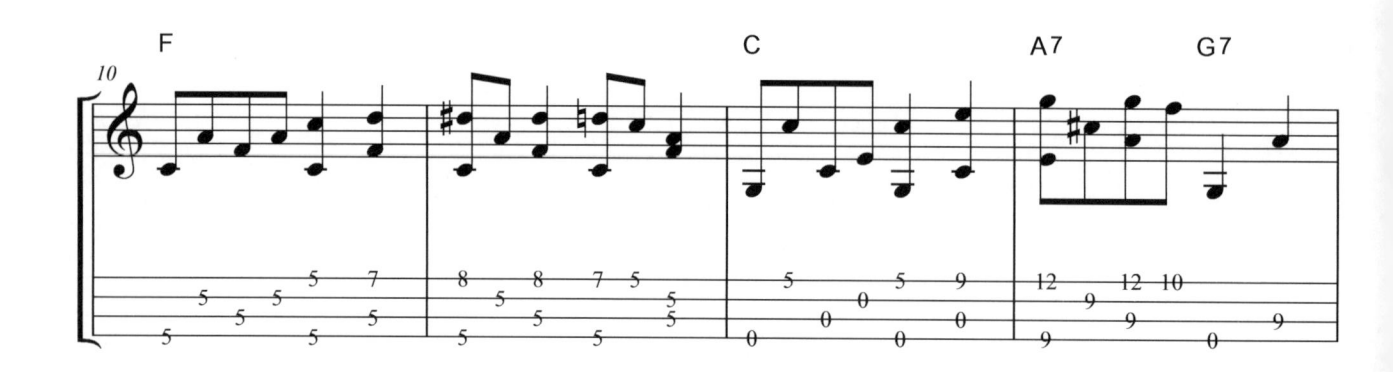

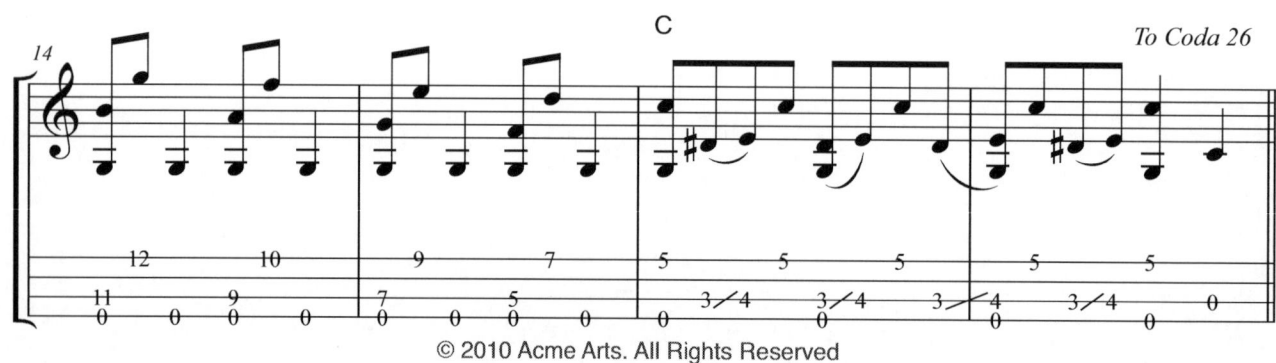

To Coda 26

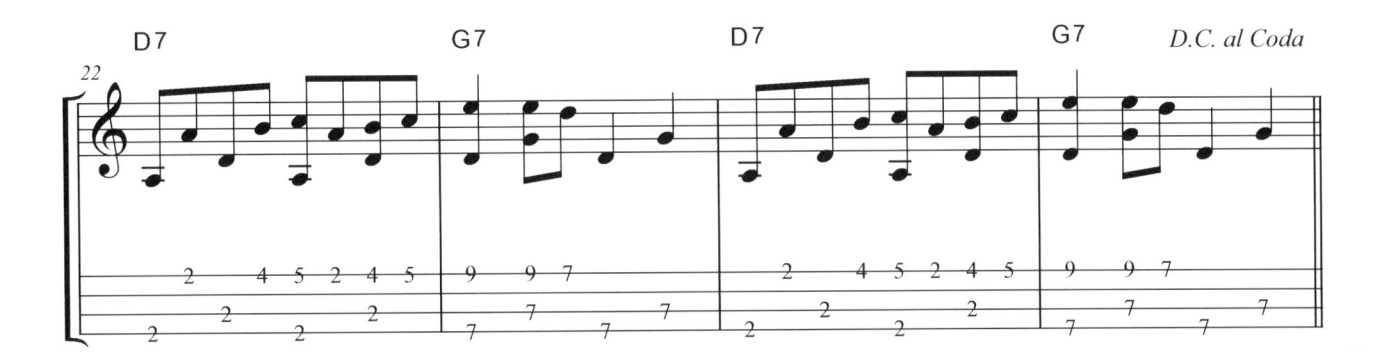

Three classic showstoppers! *Moana Chimes* and *Hula Blues* are both standards of the steel guitar repertoire. I do not recall where I learned the guitar piece *Kimo's Slack Key*, but it sure is fun to play.

Be careful with the 2/4 measures in *Moana Chimes*; just keep a steady quarter note pulse and you will be fine.

Remember to play *Hula Blues* out of the double stop fingerings.

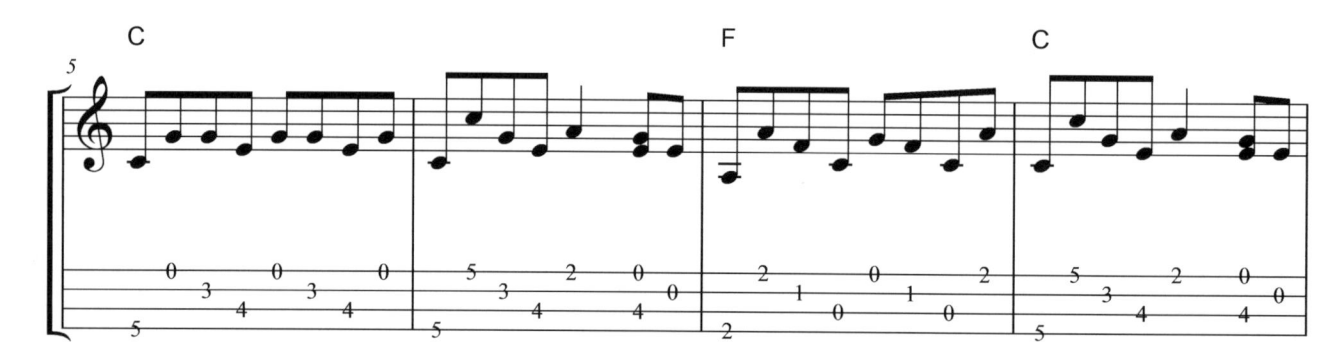

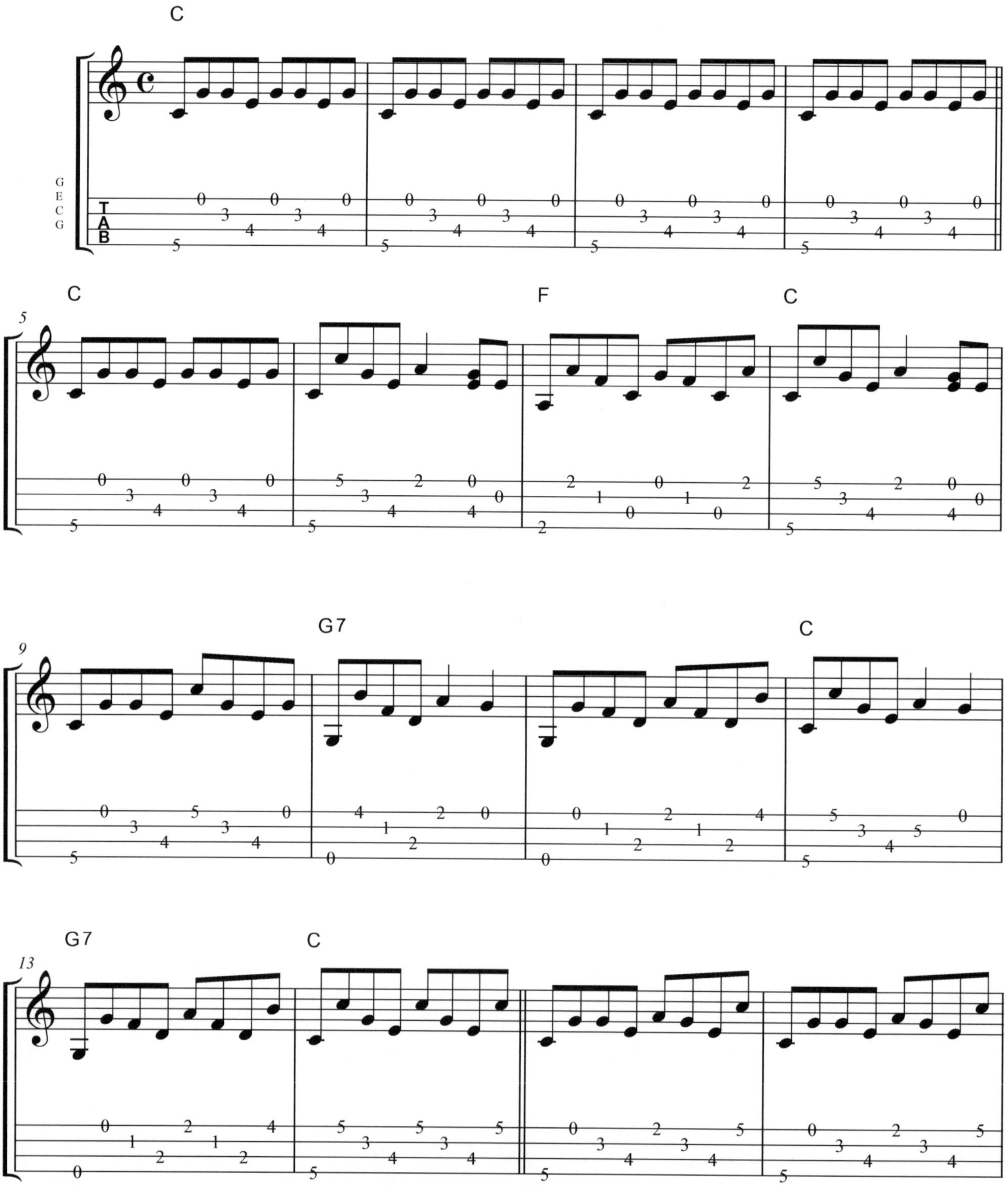

'Ukulele Dream Slack Key

in the style of Sonny Chillingworth

Low G Taropatch

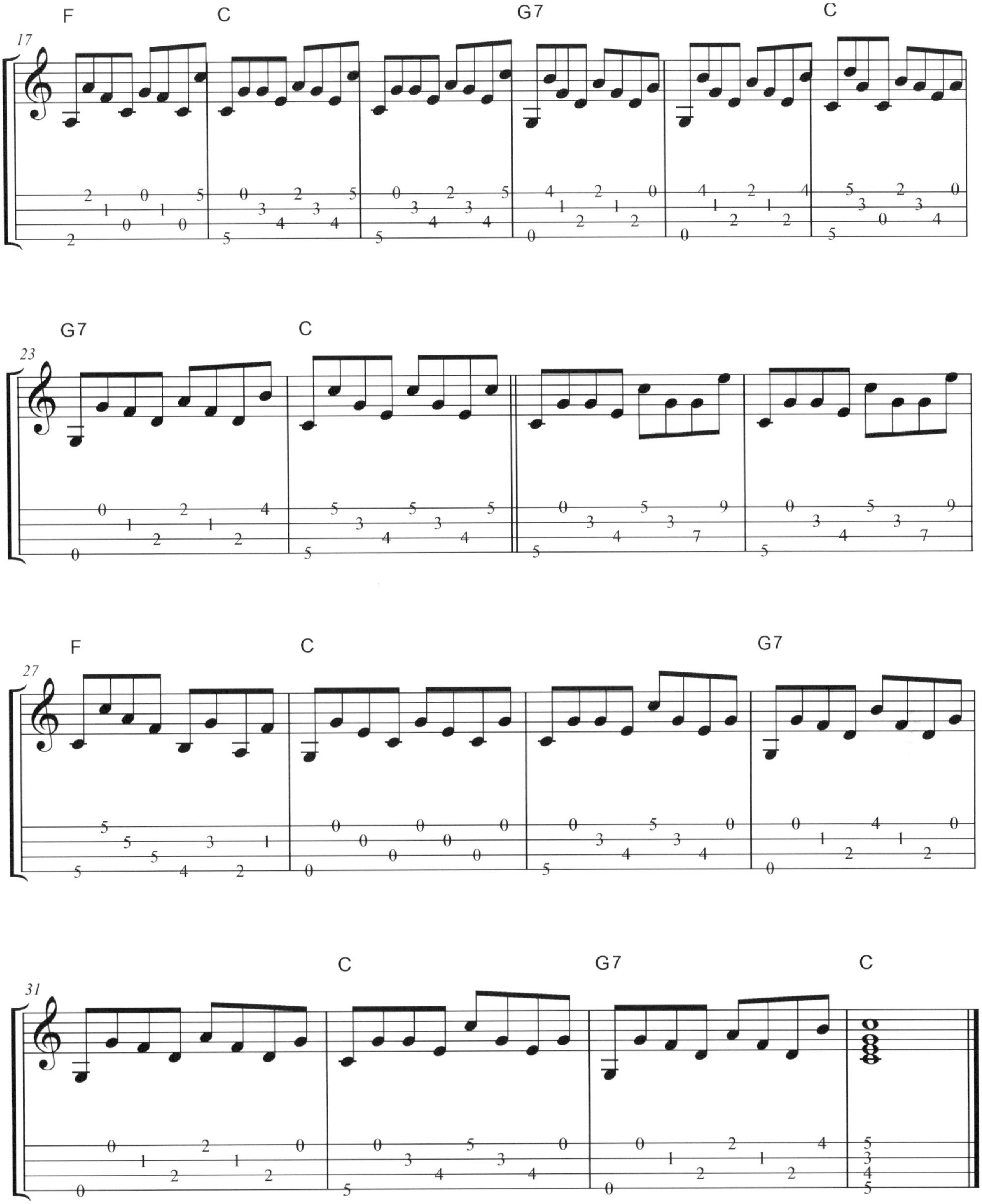

17
F
C
G7
C
23
G7
C
27
F
C
G7
31
C
G7
C

'Ukulele Dream Slack Key Performance Notes

The late Sonny Chillingworth is widely recognized as one of the true greats. Possessed of a rich baritone voice, he was a generous teacher and a virtuoso guitarist. Many of his arrangements featured the offset, syncopated bass pattern based on the *clave* rhythm common to many Big Island musicians. Perhaps it relects the Latin heritage of those early *paniolo*?

It is a difficult pattern to master, and so he wrote a pair of studies to demonstrate the style. *'Ukulele Dream Slack Key* is loosely based on that idea, and I dedicate it to Sonny.

Measures 1 - 4: The introduction will get you used to playing the clave rhythm. Hold a partial C chord and play all of the notes on the third and fourth strings with your thumb.

Measures 5 & 6: These two measures set up a basic rhythmic motif that continues throughout the song. In measure 6, hold the chord on the lowest three strings. Reach up to the fifth fret with your pinky, then reach down to the second fret with your index finger. I hold the chord as long as I can; even when playing the open second string I am still fretting both the third and fourth strings.

Playing out of the chord positions lets the notes ring and lends grace to your playing.

Measure 7: Same idea, different chord.

Measure 10: Play this out of a G7 chord shape; don't forget that you need to use your pinky for the F# on the fourth fret! I dropped the bass note on beat four just for some variety.

Measures 13 & 14: Just a basic turnaround from the G7 back to the tonic. You can suss out the fingerings for the two chords by collapsing the melody notes.

Measure 15: From here, the 10 bar form just repeats with subtle variations. Once you have played through it a few times, see what you can come up with.

Makee Ailana

James 'I'i

Low G Taropatch

Another classic from the Golden Age. Makee's Island near Waikiki was a favorite place for a late night romantic stroll.

Ahe Lau Makani
extended version

Queen Liliʻuokalani

Low G Taro Patch

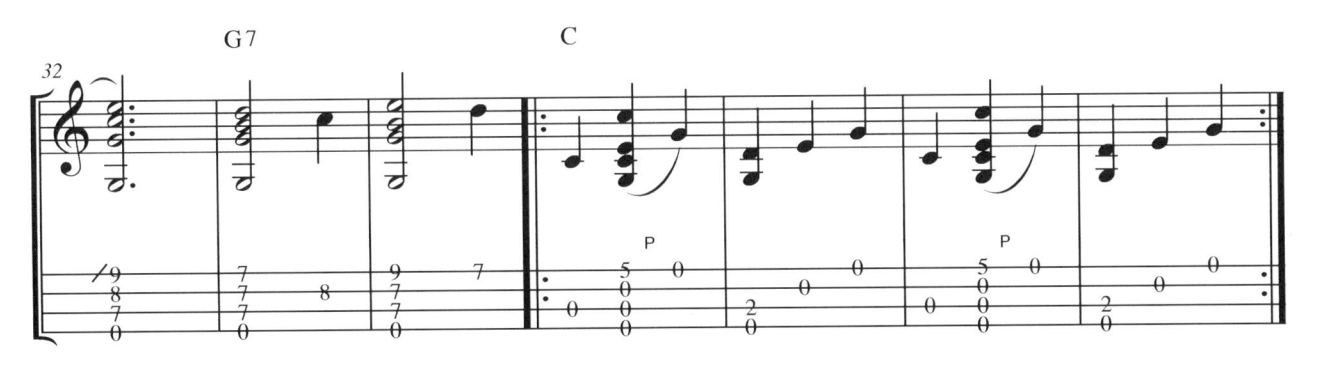

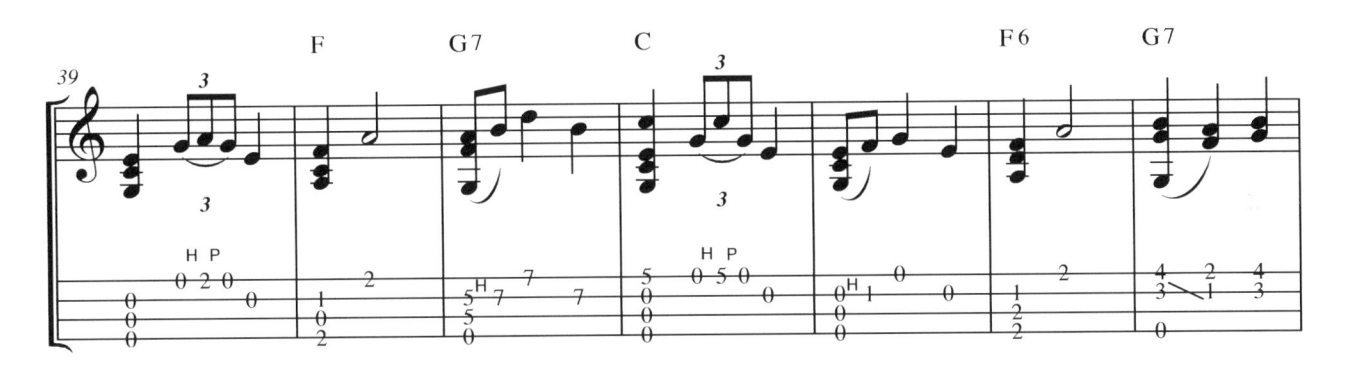

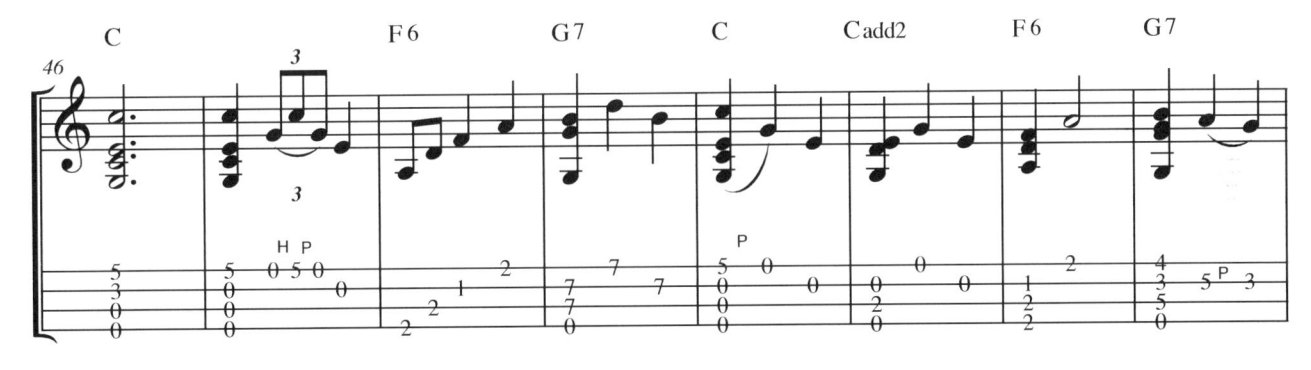

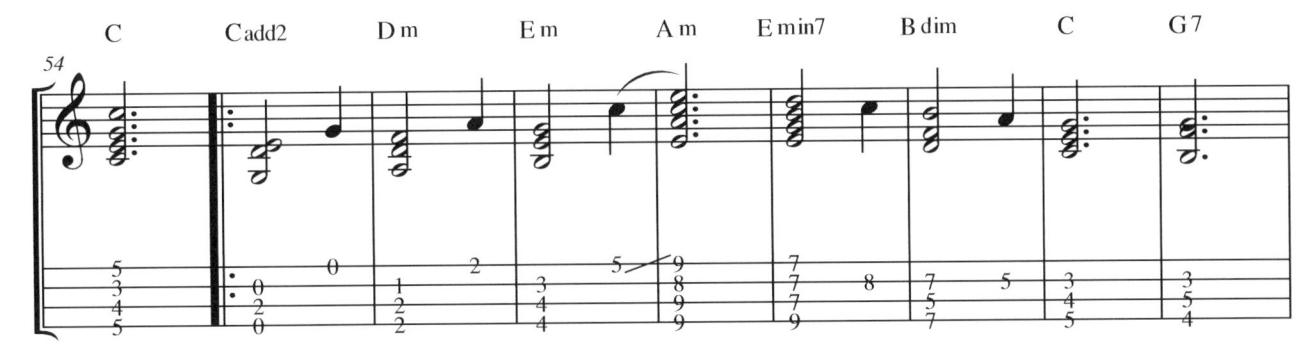

Ahe Lau Makani

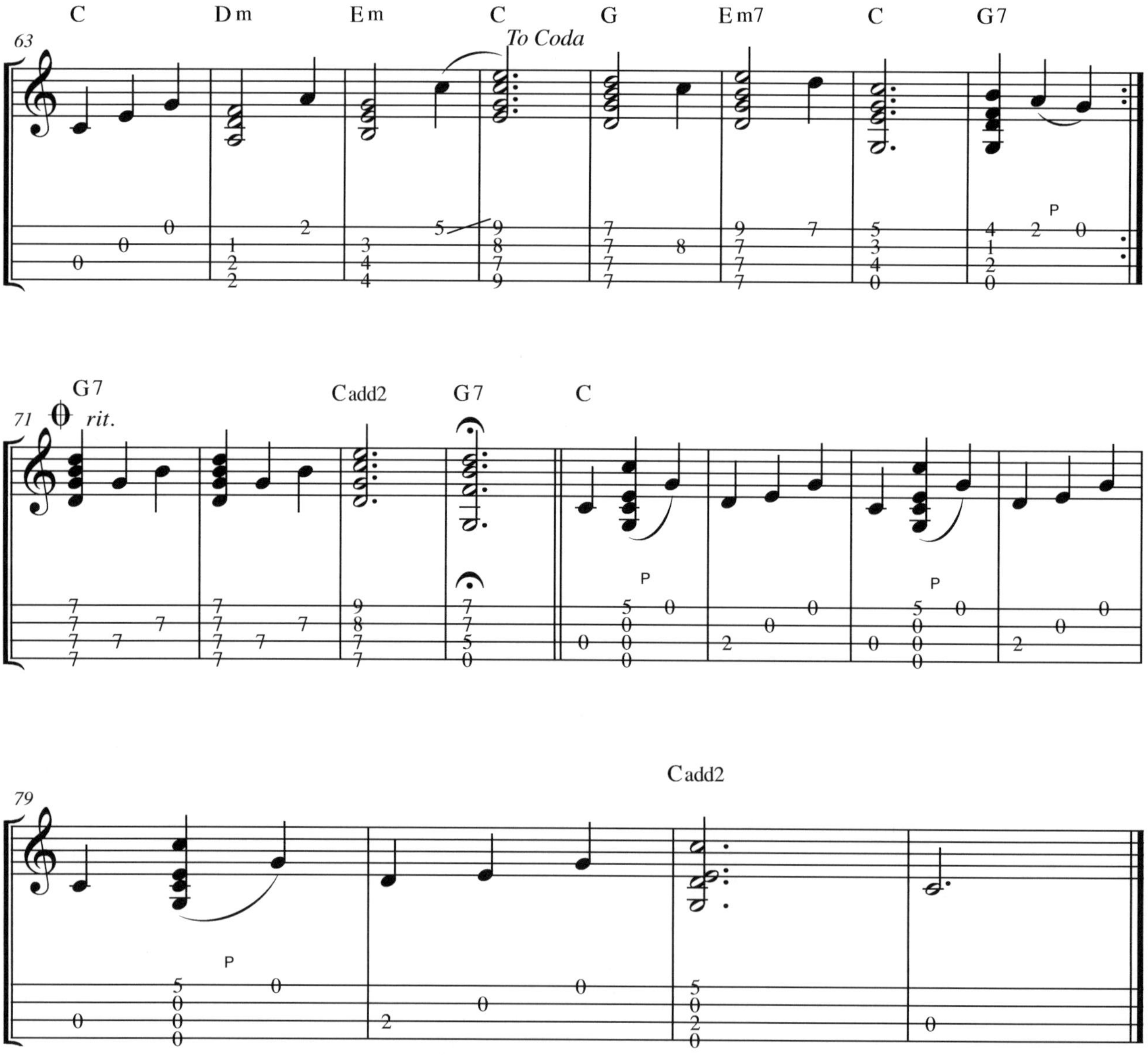
63
C
Dm
Em
C
To Coda
G
Em7
C
G7
71
G7
rit.
Cadd2
G7
C
79
Cadd2

Performance Notes

Here is another look at Queen Liliʻuokalani's waltz, this time in a fully realized arrangement.

Measures 1 - 4: This simple introduction that moves between a major chord and an add 2 suspension is reminiscent of the slack key stylings of players like Ozzie Kotani—whose masterful recording inspired this arrangement.

Measure 7: The first time through the song is the same as the version you played on page 36.

Measure 34: Rather than moving back to the start of the first melody strain at measure 7, I have restated the introduction. Short bridges open things up and keep the ear engaged. They don't have to complex, sometimes repeating one or two chords is all you need. Notice how moving from measure 34 to 35, the expected resolution to the tonic is dropped an octave.

Measure 39: Notice how the restatement of the melody has been complicated with additional slurs and grace notes. Typically, these are the kinds of things you would add spontaneously; I wrote them out here as a guide for your further explorations.

Measure 44: Sixth chords, with their indeterminate major/minor tonality, are very much a part of Hawaiian music. Introducing it here foreshadows the re-harmonization of the melody that takes place later in the arrangement.

Measure 54: The second strain of the melody harmonized with a series of ascending triads. Note that there could be alternative names for each of these chords; for example the Dm has the same tones as an F6 and the Em might also be called a C6. I chose the names I did to emphasize the upward movement of the bass line.

Measure 70: Rather than repeating the entire melody, go back to the beginning of the second strain. This alerts the listener that the arrangement is coming to a close.

Measures 54-70: On the repeat, play up to the *To Coda* marking. I might make subtle changes in picking or even substitute major chords for the ascending minors. Or maybe I wouldn't.

Measure 71: The coda starts with a simple but effective trick: where the melody would normally resolve back to the tonic after two measures of the dominant chord, I have held the resolution for two more measures. The fermata makes it even longer.

Measure 79: The by-now familiar motif used both as an introduction and a bridge now serves to bring the song to rest.

Slack Key Medley

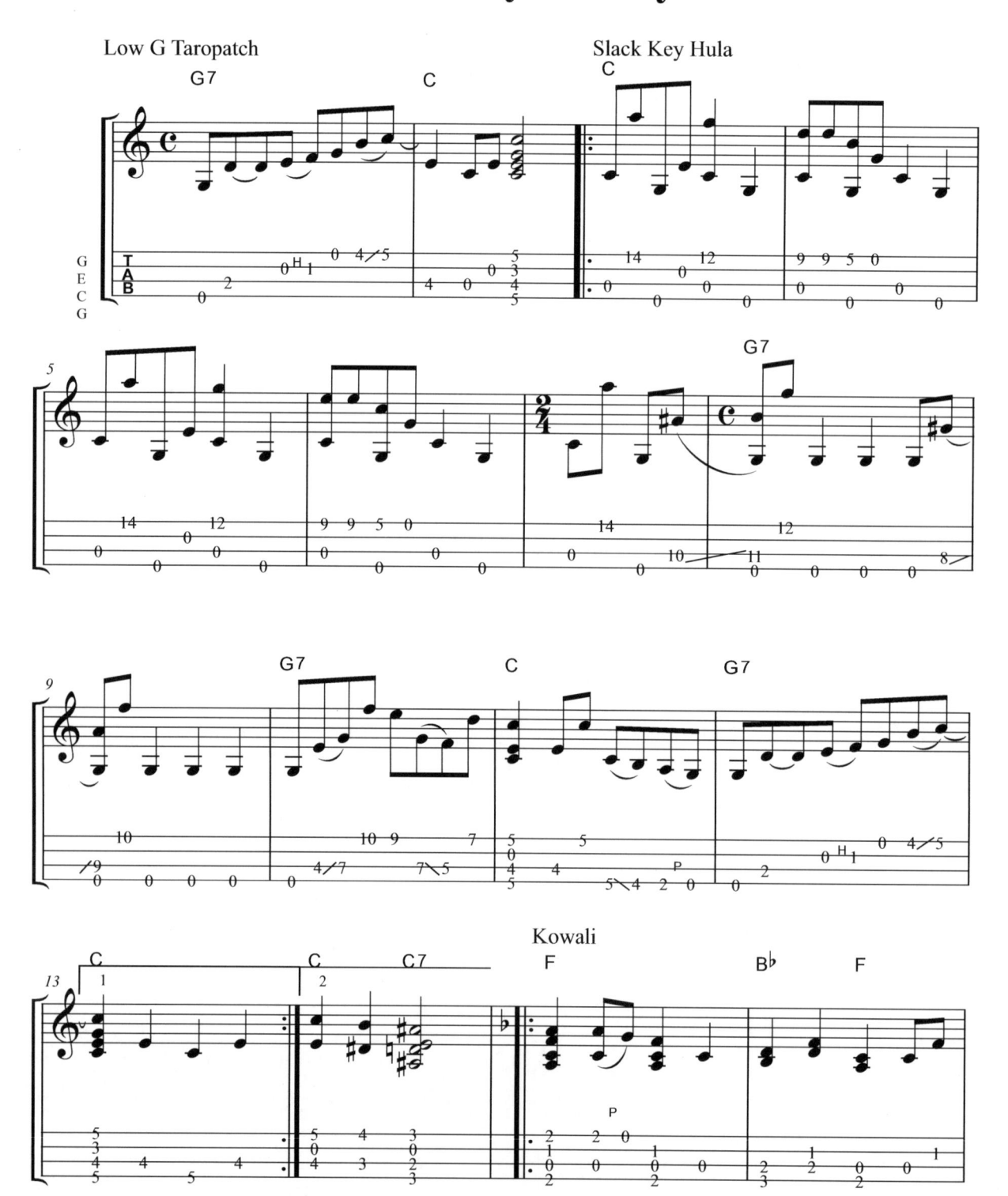

Slack Key Medley

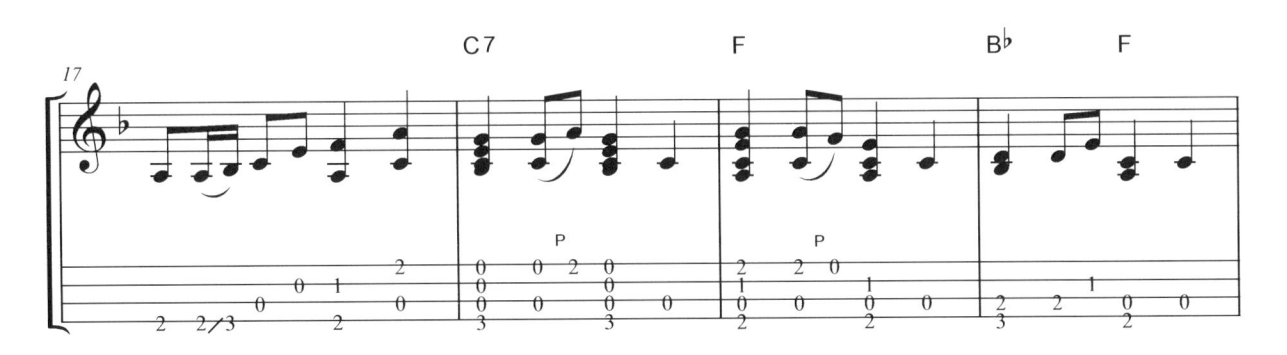

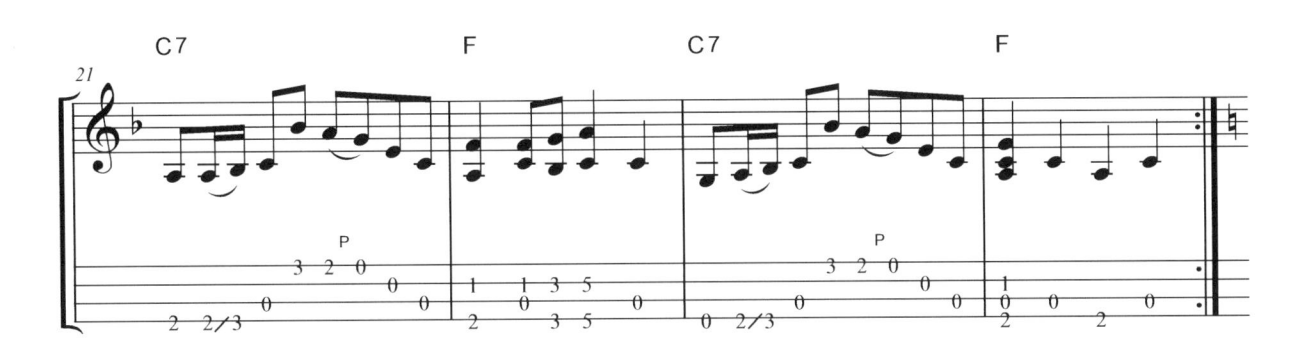

Pauoa Liko Ka Lehua

Slack Key Medley

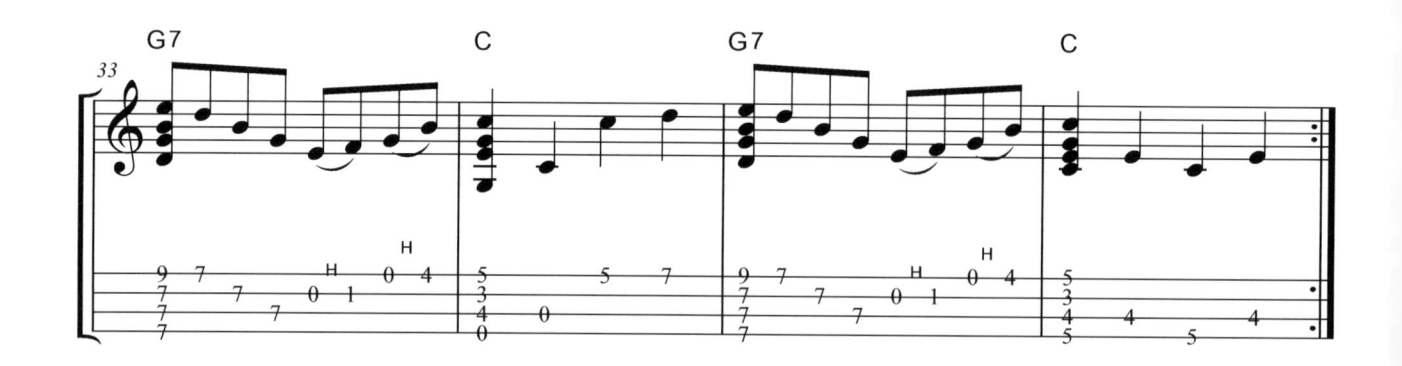

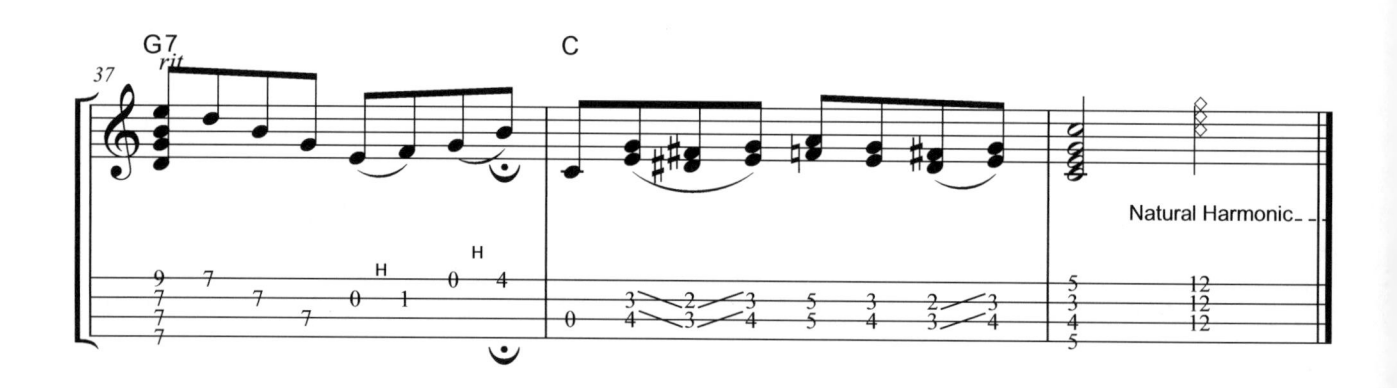

Performance Notes

Since many of Hawaiian melodies are so short, medleys are an important part of the instrumental slack key repertoire. Some players–notably Ray Kāne–are well known for their creative medleys. Here is one approach to creating your own.

Measure 3: *Slack Key Hula* is an unnamed tune associated with the great Gabby Pahinui. He recorded several different melodies under this name. Sometimes the simplest tune can be the best!

Use an alternating bass pattern with your thumb for most of the tune. Don't forget to play out of double stop positions starting on measure 7!

Measure 14: The movement from the C to the C7 chord–the dominant chord in the key of F–signals that a modulation is coming up.

Measure 15: As you have learned, Taropatch tuning is equally useful for the key of F. That makes it easy to create medleys of songs in different keys.

This is the same song you played of page 51.

Measure 25: As with the modulation from C to F, the G 7th chord alerts the listener to what is coming next.

Measure 27: Pauoa Liko Ka Lehua tells the story of a man watching the object of his heart's desire dancing the hula.

> Aia i Pauoa ka liko ka lehua
> Ka ʻiʻini pau ʻole a ka makemake
>
> There at Pauoa is the lehua bud
> My endless yearning and desire

With its full chords and large melodic jumps, it makes a nice contrast to the other two songs in the medley.

Measure 37: Another example of delaying the resolution to the tonic.

Measure 38: Here's a simple little coda figure you can use in many different places.

'Ulupalakua

traditional

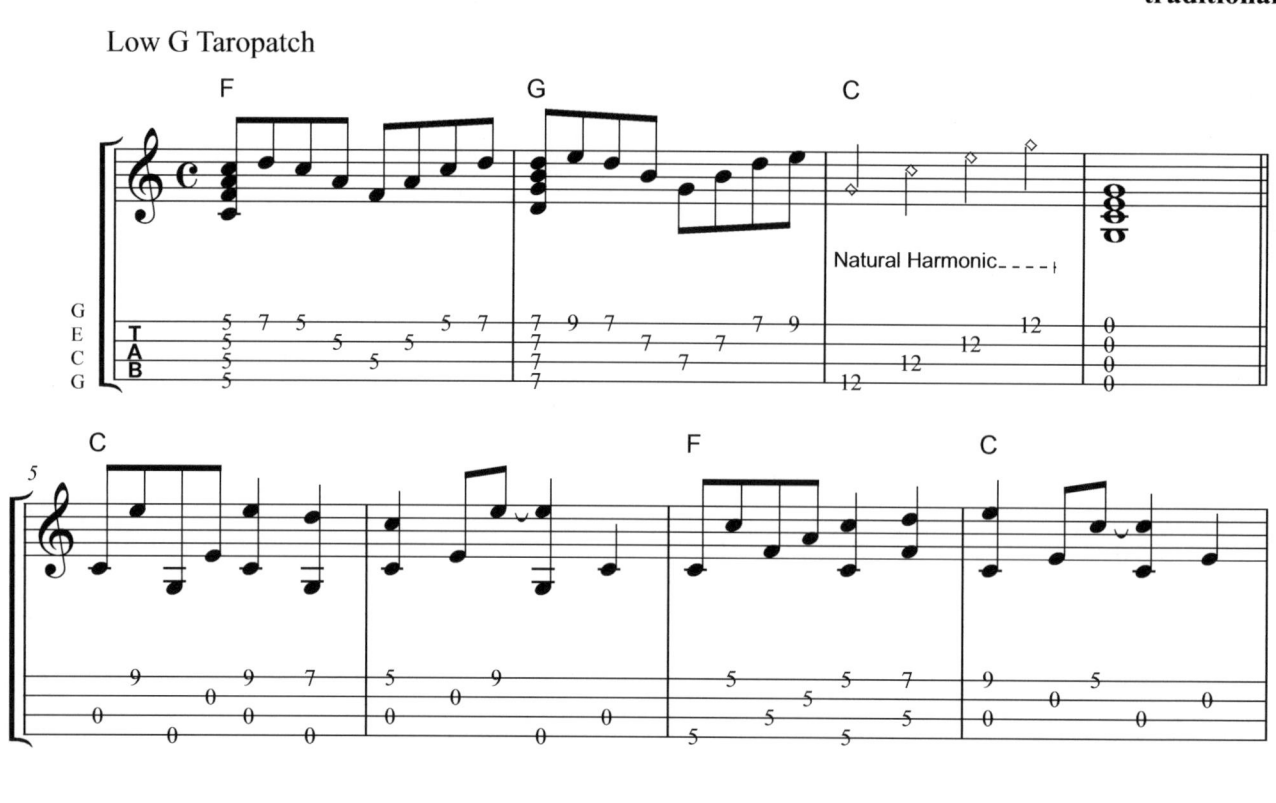

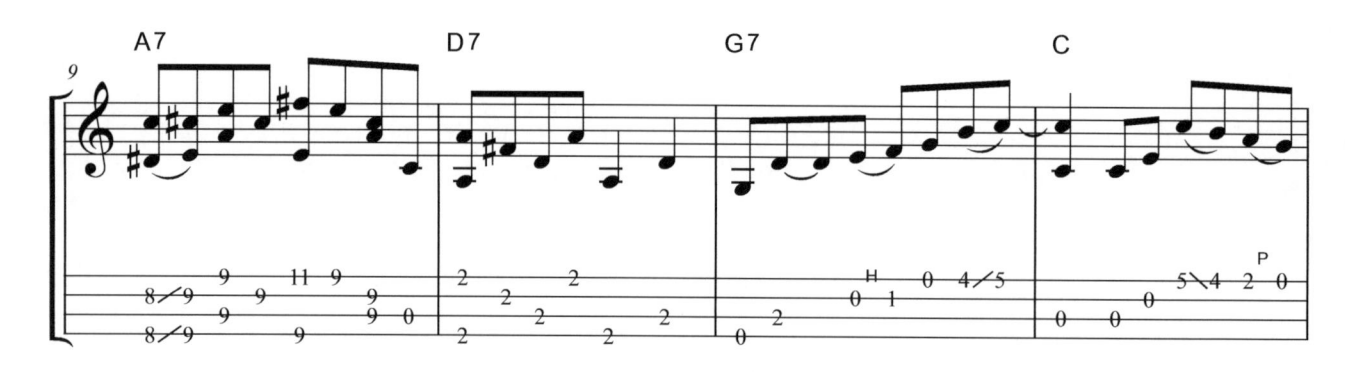

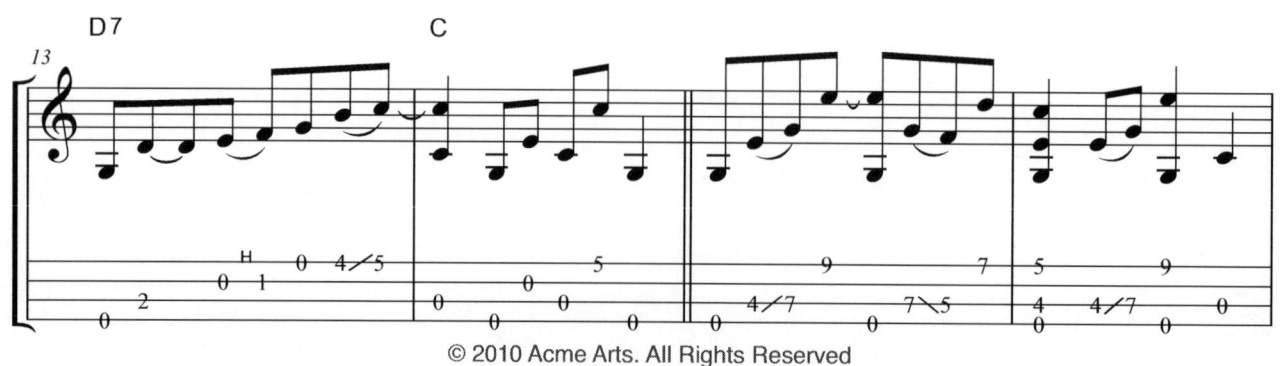

Low G Taropatch

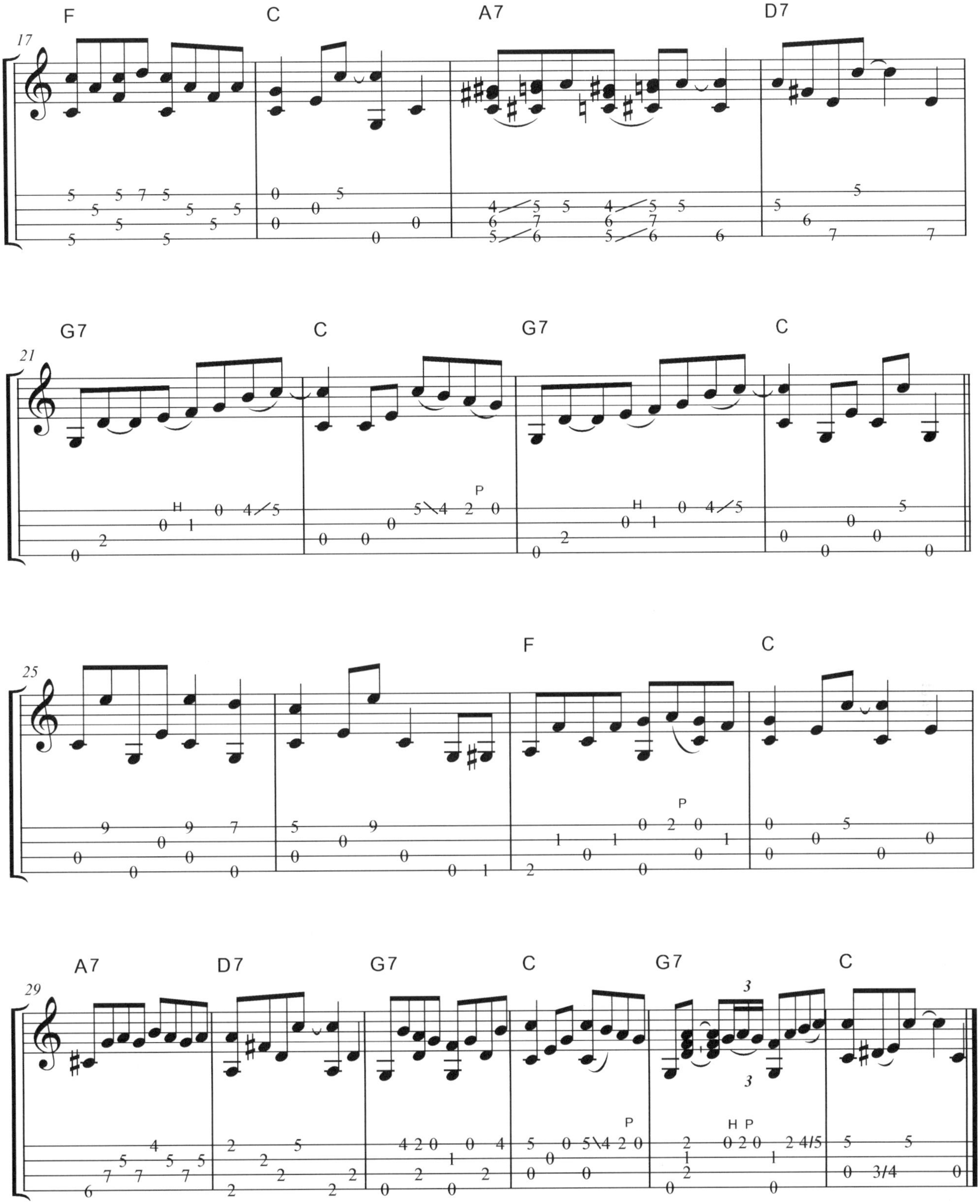

17
F C A7 D7
21
G7 C G7 C
25
F C
29
A7 D7 G7 C G7 C
3
3

'Ulupalakua Performance Notes

Like most folk musicians, Hawaiian slack key players rarely play a song the same way twice. Throughout this book I have encouraged you to try to find your own way; to go back and apply the ideas you are learning to some of the easier songs.

This arrangement of 'Ulupalakua demonstrates one approach. Take it at a brisk tempo—it is a cowboy song, after all!

Measures 1 - 4: These four measures are based on a typical, spontaneous introduction in the style of slack key players like Ray Kāne or Ledward Kaapana. Play them *rubato*, without strict time.

Measure 5: The first time through, the arrangement stays pretty close to the melody as stated in the basic version on page 14. Note that the alternating bass pattern shifts between strings depending on which harmony notes are needed. I use my thumb play the open second string in measures 6 & 8.

Measures 9 & 10: Barres across all four strings are typical of the tuning. Slide into the A chord from a half step below in measure 9, and then let go of the chord for the single open string just before the downbeat of measure 10. I "ghost" this note—that is, barely strike it. It is really more of a rhythmic accent than anything else.

Measure 15: The second time though and things start to get a little more complicated. The melody in measures 15 and 16 is hinted at by using double stop slurs.

Measure 19: Same idea as measure 9, using a different inversion of the A7 chord.

Measure 20: Collapse all of the notes in the measure to get the fingering of this chord.

Measure 22: I like to think of the descending figure as a turnaround back to the turnaround.

Measure 25: One more time! Notice that I have abandoned the melody line completely in measure 27, instead just playing out of the first position F chord.

Measure 29. Not the easiest grip, but pretty. It is an A9 chord, by the way.

Measure 34: Another typical ending lick that you can stick into many different arrangements.

If I were going to keep going, I would most likely go back to a simpler statement of the melody the next time around and then build it back up in complexity over one or two iterations.

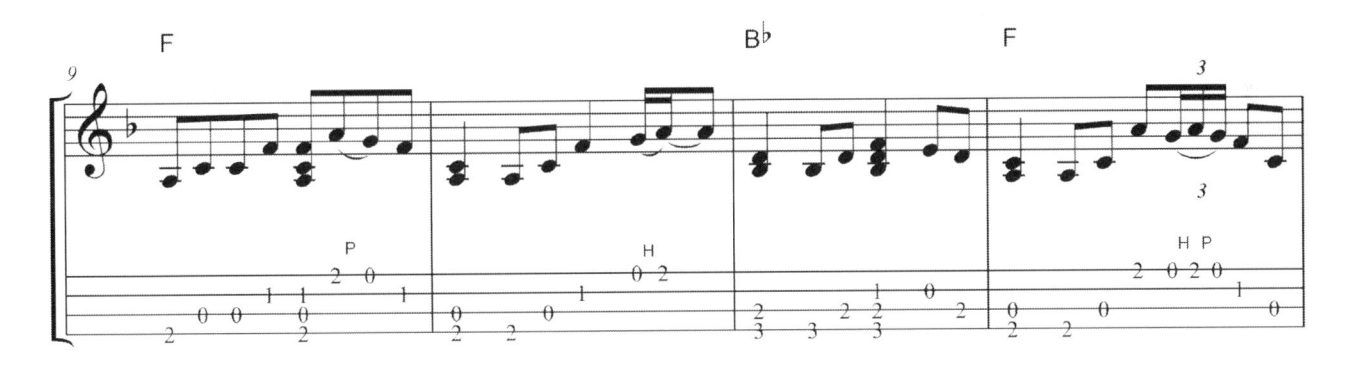

Iesu Me Ke Kanaka Waiwai
slack key
John K. Almeida

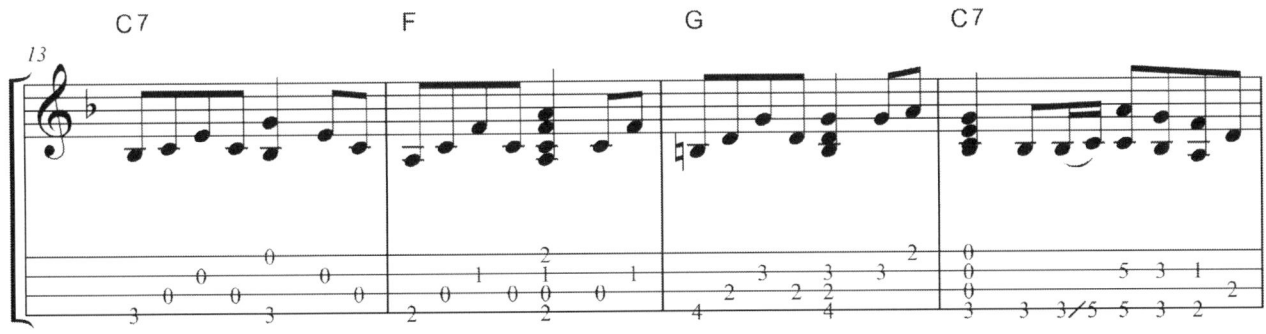

Low G Taropatch

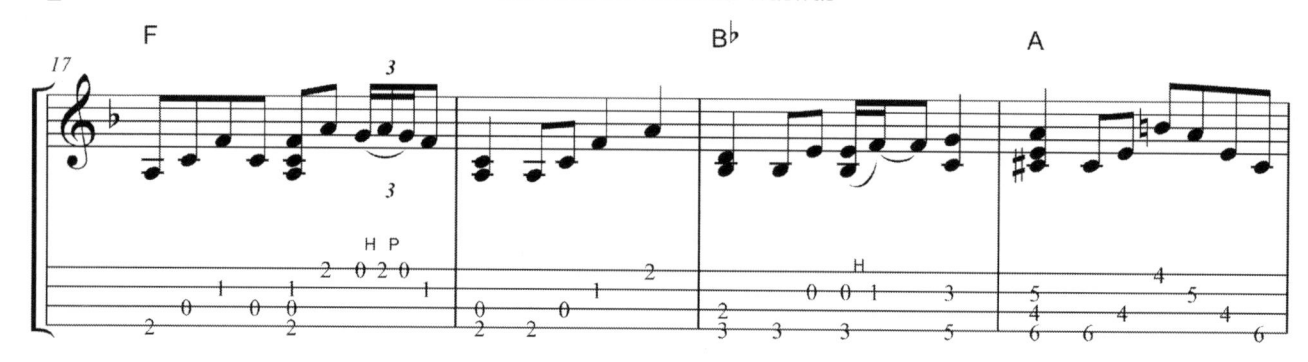

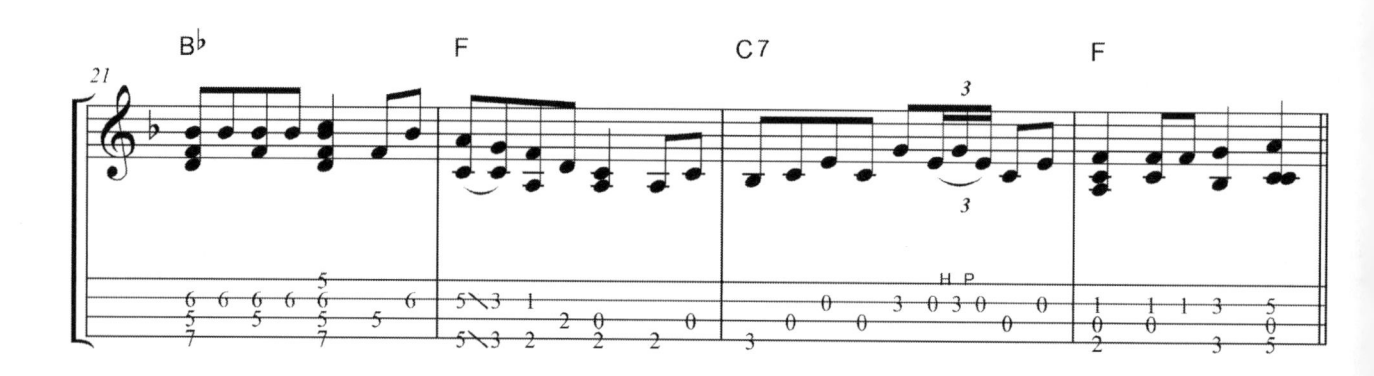

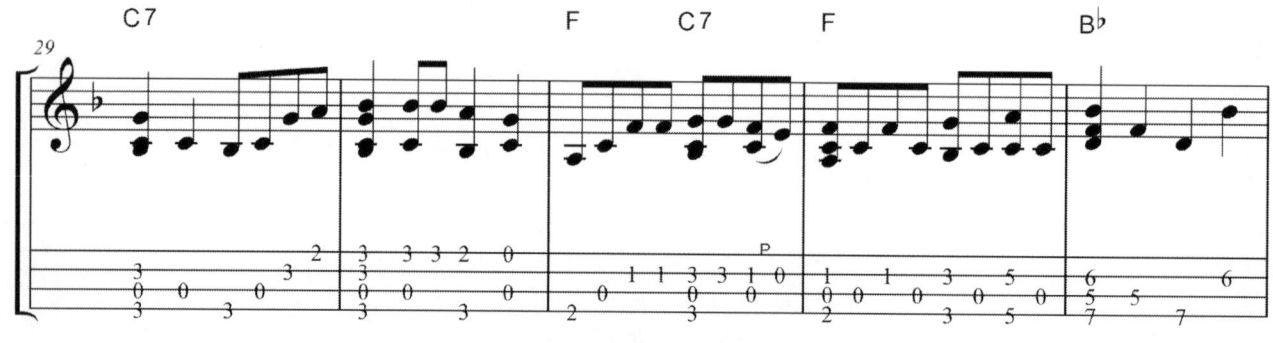

2
Iesu Me Ke Kanaka Waiwai

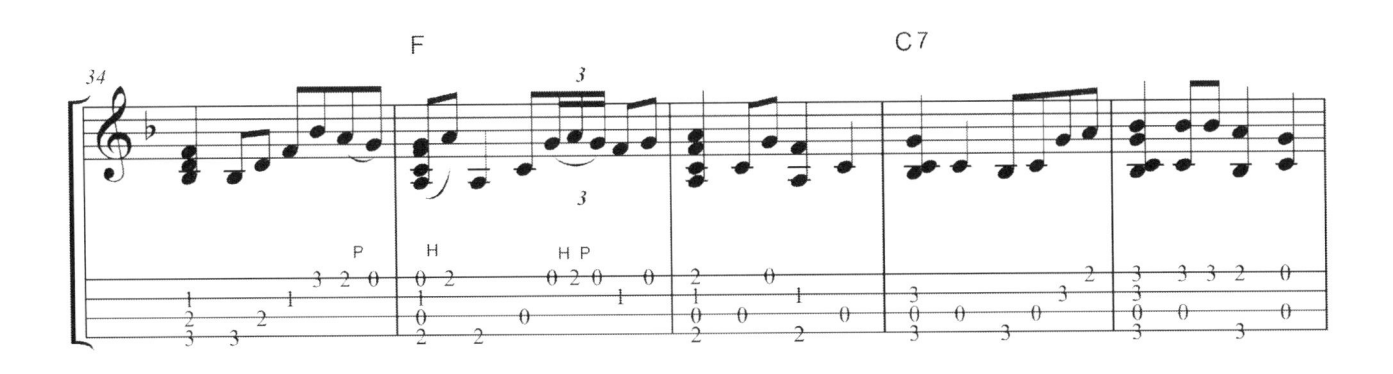

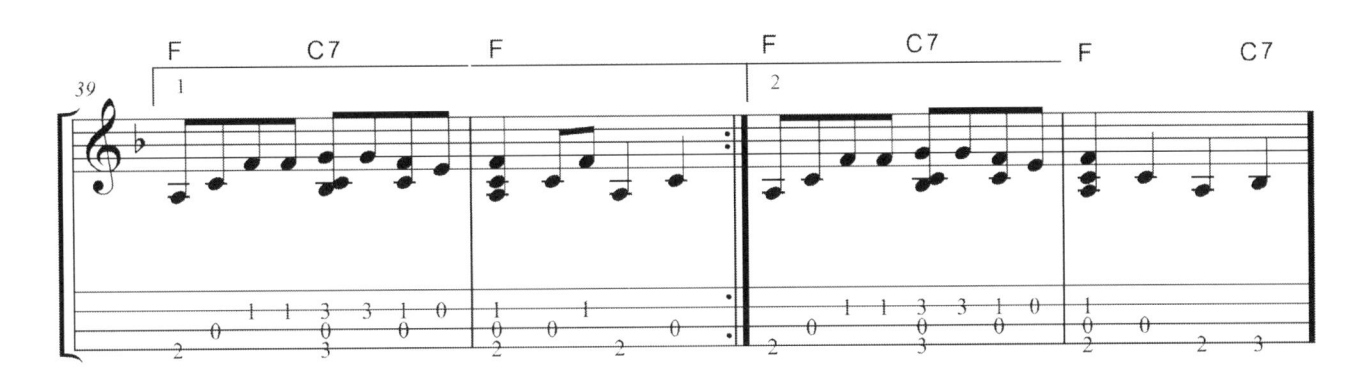

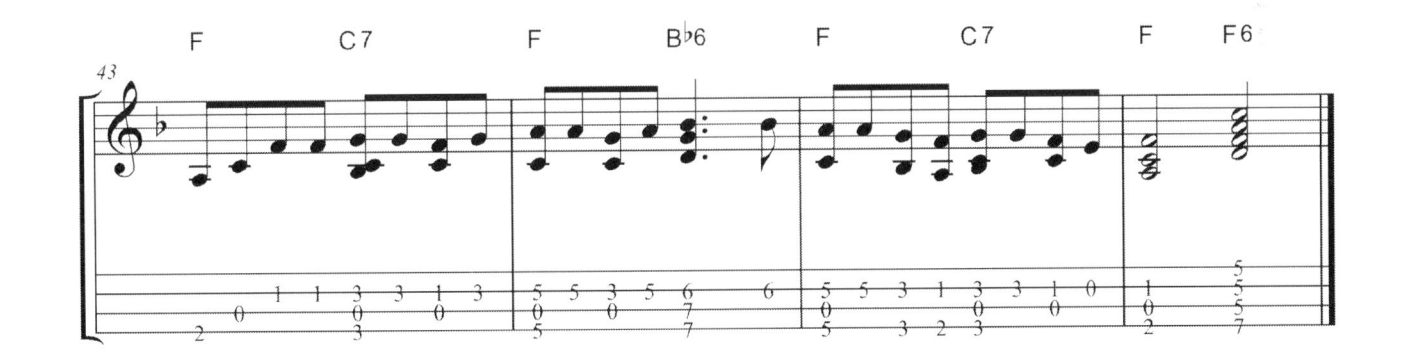

Iesu Me Ke Kanaka Waiwai

Iesu Me Ke Kanaka Waiwai Performance Notes

By now you should be pretty familiar with the ins and outs of slack key style 'ukulele. I have pulled out all the stops for this arrangement in Taropatch tuning.

Once again, rather than simply walk you through the fingerings—not that there aren't some tricky bits coming up—I want to explain some of the choices I made so you can start to create your own arrangements.

I chose F because of the melody fits well at the lower end of the fingerboard. In C, the melody goes all the way up to the 12th fret. Also, I like the chord voicings found when playing out of Taropatch in this key.

Measures 1 - 8: Another example of creating an introduction based on a simple recurring picking pattern over a basic chord progression. Although it is not notated, I would generally ritard slightly through measure 7 to alert the listener that the intro is coming to an end.

Notice the repeat sign in measure 1; you will be coming back here after awhile.

Measure 9: The melody just falls out of the F chord shape, with out any large reaches or position shifts. It is very simple to add slurs such as the pull-off in measure 9, quick hammer-on in measure 10, or triplet figure in measure 12.

Measure 25: The second strain begins sparse and simple to create a contrast from some of the complexity I added in earlier measures. It won't stay simple long.

Measure 39: After playing the first ending, go back and play the intro again to break things up a bit before restating the melody.

By now you ought to have enough tricks up your sleeve to know how to find your own variations the next time through.

Measure 41: Another example of creating a coda by delaying the resolution. In this case I created motif based on the last two measures of the song, moving it up the neck through the tonic, dominant and sub-dominant chords.

Hana Hou

Many concerts in Hawai'i end with the audience shouting these words: *Hana hou!* "Do it again!" "Don't stop, play another one!"

So here is one last arrangement for you. An encore, if you will. It is a song you have played before; this time with even more twists and turns and slippry licks. Just the thing to wow the crowd before you take your bow and leave the stage.

Thank you for sticking with the book for this long. I hope you have had as much fun playing this music as I do.

The next time we meet, bring your 'ukulele and lets play a few tunes.

Mark Kailana Nelson

Now turn the page, and ***"Hana Hou!"***

'Ukulele Slack Key #1
Extended Version

Mark Kailana Nelson

Low G Taropatch tuning

Ukulele Slack Key #1

Ukulele Slack Key #1

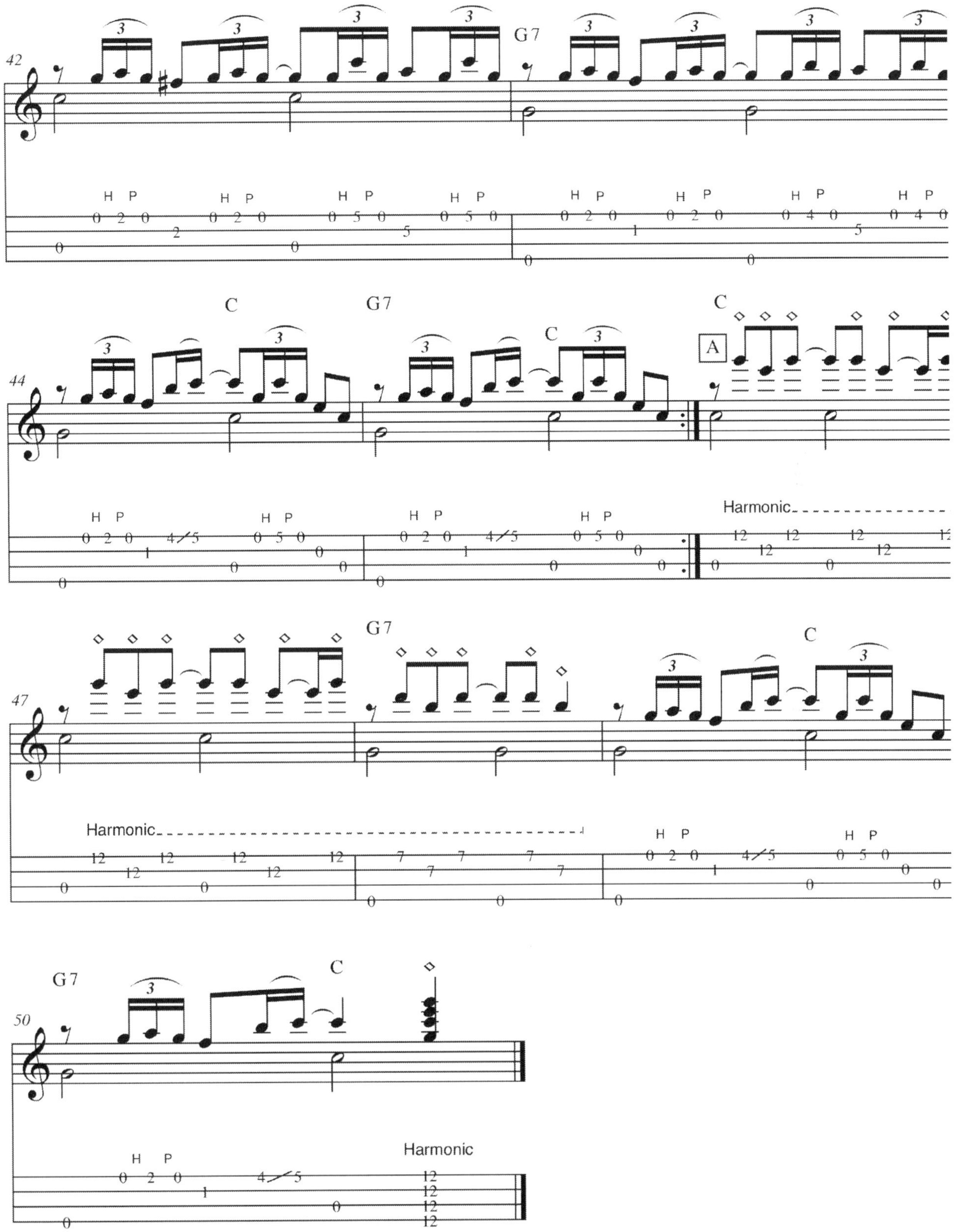

42
G7
H P
C
G7
C
44
A
Harmonic
47
G7
C
Harmonic
50
G7
C
Harmonic

Guide to Hawaiian Pronunciation

The Hawaiians had no written alphabet until one was created by the missionaries slightly over 150 years ago. To someone unfamiliar with the language, the multiple vowels and long words may appear daunting at first. Just remember to pronounce every letter and to break up long words into smaller parts, and you'll do fine.

Most glossaries will tell you that there are twelve letters in the Hawaiian alphabet: the five vowels A, E, I, O and U; and seven consonants: H, K, L, M, N, P and W. This is OK as far as it goes, but the spoken language is considerably richer. Certain sounds were difficult for English speakers to shoehorn into the common alphabet; one confusing example is the letter W. Depending on where it falls in a word, and depending on where in the Islands the speaker lives, this letter may sound like a V, like a W, or like something in between.

Vowels are pronounced similar to Spanish. The macron changes the vowel slightly, making it sound longer.

    a as in far
    ā as in father
    e as in bet
    ē like ay in pay
    i, ī like ee in see
    o ō as in sole
    u, ū like oo in moon

The vowel pairs: ai, ae, ao, au, ei, eu, iu, and oi. Pronounce each letter individually, with a slight stress on the first. The second letter is pronounced softly. They differ from the English diphthong; so *maikaʻi* (good) is ma-ee-KA-ʻee, not MY-KY.

The consonants are pronounced almost as they are in English, but generally softer.

W is a special case:
    following **i** or **e**, pronounce it as a soft **v**.
    as the initial letter, or following **a**; pronounce it as either a **w** or a soft **v**.
    following **u** and **o**; usually pronounced as **w**, but sometimes as a soft **v**.

The **ʻokina** (ʻ) is another difficult sound for English speakers to grasp. This symbol represents a glottal stop, an abrupt cessation of breath similar to the sound between the words in the exclamation: Uh-oh! The **ʻokina** is a consonant, failure to pronounce it changes the meaning of the word, such as *pau* = finished, and paʻu = soot, smudge.

As a general rule, accent the next to the last syllable in short words. Break up longer words into pieces to help find the stress; so *Lililehua* becomes Lili - Lehua.

Resources

Songbooks
He Mele Aloha: A Hawaiian Song Book, Carol Wilcox, ed. 'Oli'oli Productions, 2003
The Queen's Songbook, Hui Hānai 1999
King's Book of Hawaiian Melodies, Centerbrook Publishing 2001
Nā Mele o Hawai'i Nei, Elbert & Mahoe, University of Hawai'i Press, 1970

Websites
www.Huapala.org – Extensive collection of Hawaiian song lyrics and translations. Some have MIDI files.

http://mele.home.att.net/home.htm - Online site with MIDI files of the songs in the **He Mele Aloha** songbook.

http://web.mac.com/halaumohalailima/HMI/Waihona_Mele.html - An ever-expending set of essays featuring the stories behind Hawaiian songs.

www.mele.com - an excellent source of both recordings and books.

www.TaroPatch.net – The on-line community for lovers of slack key and Hawaiian culture

www.AlohaMusicCamp.com – Study 'ukulele in the land of its birth! The Aloha Camps are week-long immersions into the music and culture of Hawai'i.

Recordings:
The best way to learn slack key is by listening. Although both musicians play in standard 'ukulele tuning, recordings by Herb Ohta, Jr. and Keoki Kahumuku are highly recommended. Sadly, slack key uke virtuoso Sheldon Brown has only one recording, a long out of print LP with his band the Wai'ehu Sons. It shows up on eBay from time to time, and is well worth finding

In addition, search out recordings by these great Hawaiian slack key guitarists:

Gabby Pahinui, Sonny Chillingworth, Ray Kāne, Ledward Kaapana, Keola Beamer, Ozzie Kotani, George Kuo, Cyril Pahinui, James "Bla" Pahinui, Moses Kahumoku and George Kahumoku, Jr., John Keawe and many others.

Mark's "Funtime Uke-A-Rama" CD includes *Iesu Me Ke Kanaka Waiwai* and *'Ukulele Slack Key #1*.
Mark's "Learn to Play Fingerstyle Solos for 'Ukulele" contains a number of Hawaiian songs, including several arranged slack key style.

Audio and MIDI files for all of the songs in this book are available for download at www.Mark-o.com

Mark is proud to endorse **Po Mahina 'Ukulele and Guitars**, made by Big Island luthier Dennis Lake.
PO Box 845
Na'alehu, HI 96772
www.Konaweb.com/Mahina

Mark is an enthusiastic endorser of **Mya-Moe Resonator 'Ukulele**.
18 Forbes Road, White Salmon, WA 98672
www.MyaMoeUkulele.com

Mark Kailana Nelson

Multi-instrumentalist Mark Nelson has carved a unique niche for himself as an entertainer, musician and educator. His deep love and understanding of traditional music led him to the mastery of several different musical idioms, ranging from old time western music to Celtic to Hawaiian. In a career that began well before he was able to drive, he has performed everywhere from street corners to hay barns to festivals to the concert stage in the US, Europe and Canada. He once worked as a banjo playing gorilla in Dublin, but that's a different story.

Growing up near the beach in Southern California, Mark was surrounded by the music and culture of the Hawaiian Islands. His love of *kī hō'alu*, slack key guitar, led him to travel to Hawai'i and study with some of the masters. This in turn has led to a deep friendship with noted Hawaiian musician Keola Beamer and his illustrious family – Aunty Nona Beamer gave Mark his Hawaiian name, *Kailana* (Floating on the Sea). Keola and Mark have collaborated on numerous projects, including a book, *Learn to Play Hawaiian Slack Key Guitar*. Together they host The Aloha Music Camp, a week-long immersion in the music and culture of Hawai'i held on the Island of Hawai'i.

Mark is proud to endorse Po Mahina 'Ukulele, made by Big Island luthier Dennis Lake, and resonator 'Ukulele from Mya-Moe of Washington.

Mark lives in Southern Oregon's Applegate Valley with his wife Annie and various furred and finned friends, where he divides his time between studio work, writing, and watching the trees grow.

Selected Discography

Funtime Uke-A-Rama
Ke Kukima Polinahe
Old Time Hawaiian Slack Key Guitar
The Water is Wide
autumn…
The Faery Hills
After the Morning
The Rights of Man

Books

Old Time Hawaiian Slack Key Guitar
Learn to Play Hawaiian Slack Key Guitar
Learn to Play Fingerstyle Solos for 'Ukulele
Ke Kukima Polinahe: Hawaiian Music For Dulcimer
Favorite Old-Time American Songs for Appalachian Dulcimer
The Complete Collection of Celtic Music for Appalachian Dulcimer
Fiddle Tunes for Dulcimer: The Rights of Man

Mark Nelson
Acme Arts
PO Box 967
Jacksonville, OR 97530
www.Mark-o.com

Printed in Great Britain
by Amazon.co.uk, Ltd.,
Marston Gate.